A **FALCON** GUIDE ®

Touring

COLORADO
HOT SPRINGS

Carl Wambach

FALCON GUIDE ®

GUILFORD, CONNECTICUT
HELENA, MONTANA

AN IMPRINT OF THE GLOBE PEQUOT PRESS

A FALCON GUIDE®

Falcon and FalconGuide are registered trademarks of Morris Book Publishing, LLC.

Illustrations by Peter Grosshauser.

All black-and-white photos by Carl Wambach unless otherwise noted.

Library of Congress Cataloging-in-Publication Data

Wambach, Carl, 1955–
     Touring Colorado hot springs / Carl Wambach.
        p.   cm. — (A FalconGuide)
     Includes bibliographical references (p.   ) and index.
     ISBN-13: 978-1-56044-736-8
     ISBN-10: 1-56044-736-2 (paperback)
        1. Hot springs—Colorado—Guidebooks. 2. Colorado—Guidebooks.
    I. Title. II. Series : Falcon guide.
     GB1198.3.C6W25 1999
     551.2'3'09788—dc21   99-12547
                                                CIP

Manufactured in the United States of America
First Edition/Fifth Printing

♻ Text pages printed on recycled paper.

To buy books in quantity for corporate use
or incentives, call **(800) 962–0973, ext. 4551,**
or e-mail **premiums@GlobePequot.com.**

ACKNOWLEDGMENTS

Like putting together a complicated toy on Christmas Eve, this book is an assembly project. It is a composite of ideas, reference research, uncounted miles on the road, gritty hours in front of a computer screen, and more appreciation for the sheer complexity of putting it all together. The glue that binds it is the support of friends and loved ones along the way. They have my warmest appreciation and deserve partial credit for the completed effort.

It was my sturdy and reliable friend Brendan Beatty who catalyzed the launch of this project when he introduced me to his climbing friend Randall Green, at that time the guidebook editor for Falcon Publishing. Randall has the smooth demeanor and reassuring sense of integrity that serves him well climbing frighteningly steep rocks, but which also made writing this book suddenly seem quite appealing and achievable.

For those who have given their unwavering support, I offer this finished book as my humble gift in return.

CONTENTS

MAP LEGEND

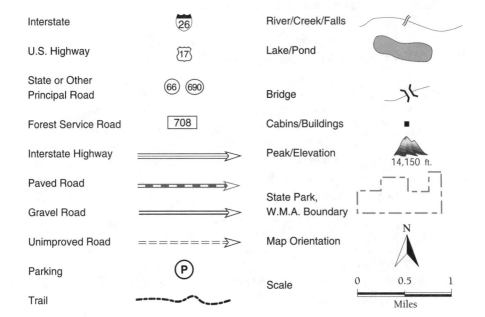

Interstate	26	River/Creek/Falls	
U.S. Highway	17	Lake/Pond	
State or Other Principal Road	66 690	Bridge	
Forest Service Road	708	Cabins/Buildings	
Interstate Highway	⟹	Peak/Elevation	14,150 ft.
Paved Road	⟹	State Park, W.M.A. Boundary	
Gravel Road	⟹		
Unimproved Road	=======⟹	Map Orientation	N
Parking	P		
Trail		Scale	0 0.5 1 Miles

OVERVIEW MAP

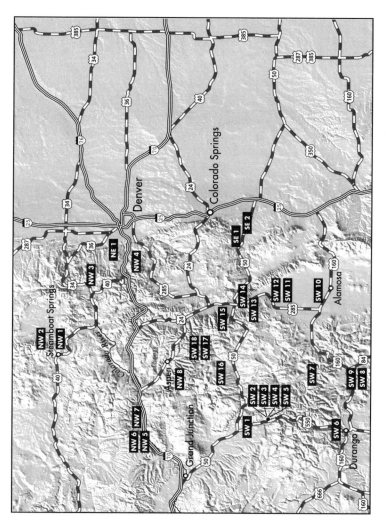

INTRODUCTION

IN THE BEGINNING

Hot springs are kind of a "serendipity thing." The dictionary defines *serendipity* as luck or good fortune—as in finding something of value by accident. I hope the maps and directions in this guidebook will make it easy for you to find the springs discussed here, but long before there were guidebooks, there was hot-springs serendipity. By that I mean there were animals and people who encountered the springs when they were looking for something else. Our early ancestors were not recreational hot-potters who, guidebooks in hand, went about looking for great new places to relax and commune with nature. Most often they were searching for a quick meal to dig up, kill, or steal when they happened upon a pool of hot water bubbling up out of the earth. Tossing off their animal-skin loincloths and jumping in probably never crossed their minds. For you, serendipity may have just taken place, if you picked up this guidebook and are about to discover the sublime, delightful world of Colorado's hot springs. Read on, and I'll show you why.

"Something for everyone" is a phrase as trite and overstated as the "new and improved" slogan, a favorite of Madison Avenue advertising agencies, but when used to describe nature's hot springs, those words come close to being true. Mother Nature has drawn us a hot bath in myriad forms and locations around the world, and flatters the American West with a grand assortment. There are some two thousand hot springs in the United States, most of them in the West where geologic activity is most prevalent. In Colorado there are tiny seeps of water oozing from cracks in the rocks, streamlets just barely warm enough to warrant the Colorado Geological Survey's designation as geothermal sites. You can also find springs that gush 3.5 million gallons of hot water every day into a pool big enough to hold most South Dakota farm towns. The majority of Colorado's hot springs are somewhere in between these extremes, but it is their diversity that makes this book so handy, and exploring the hot springs so much fun.

A Little Background

Hot springs are constantly changing, and I'll give you a little background on what a hot springs is and where it came from shortly, but you might be surprised to know that hot water springs that existed for centuries can suddenly disappear, while hot springs can appear suddenly—without human intervention— in places that have never seen a drop of naturally heated groundwater. For the most part, hot springs are a result of the natural cycle of water as it moves over and through the earth's crust. A thermal site that you visit today has probably been around for at least a few centuries, and been appreciated by an enormous variety of microbes, birds, small animals, large beasts, and lately, we humans. We have even created a few thermal flows of our own by drilling into the crust of the earth in search of fluids decidedly more black, gooey, and flammable. More about that later, too.

Do you need to know what a hot springs is in order to enjoy one? No more than you need to understand how your automobile engine works in order to drive your car, but you may find that knowing something about both will enhance your appreciation and keep you from experiencing needless troubles. Fortunately for you, I do not plan to explain how your car engine works, and certainly will not tell you how to drive it. Well, maybe I might in the heat of a 5:00 P.M. traffic jam. I will give you a little background on what creates a typical hot spring and suggest that if you are intrigued by the geology of it all, you will certainly find other sources more comprehensive. Refer to the references in Appendix B, at the back of this book.

Hot springs are part of the hydrologic cycle, which includes water from the earth's surface that becomes atmospheric, precipitates, and ends up on or below the surface again. There are numerous complexities and variations in the process that exceed the scope of what I wish to discuss here, and probably go beyond what you want to know just now, so consider this a (very) short course on hydrogeology.

When water in the oceans and lakes (surface water) evaporates through the effects of the sun and wind, it is carried into the atmosphere as vapor. Water vapor is all around you as humidity, even when you cannot feel or see it. When that vapor cools, either because it rises high enough above the earth to lose its heat or because it is acted upon by something as simple as the sun setting, it can form visible moisture vapor—for example, a cloud. At some point that vapor cools enough to make precipitation, which can be in the form of rain, sleet, snow, or cats and dogs, depending on how cool the ambient temperature is. When that water, frozen or otherwise, precipitates, it usually drops right back into an ocean, simply because so much water covers the earth already.

Some moisture hitting the ground eventually flows over the surface into streams and rivers, but much of it is soaked up by the soil and thirsty plants. The water that makes its way into the subsoil ends up as part of an aquifer, or fluid trapped in underground reservoirs of wet gravel. That's a simplification, of course, but you get the idea. In some areas the water filters down deeper into the earth because there are no impermeable layers of clay or bedrock, and it begins to feel some heat. The center of our planet is mostly molten rock, a legacy of very hot materials that date back to the very formation of the earth. In some places, such as western Colorado, there are pockets of molten magma surprisingly close to the surface, where they can heat water that has percolated down from above. Under pressure, water can exceed the normal boiling point of 212 degrees F by quite a margin, but that information may be best left to earth scientists and wildcat drillers. The rest of us can just try to remember that, deep underground, the heat from the planet's molten rocks gives birth to the hot springs in which we can soak our bones.

Seeking out natural fault lines and fissures in the rock, the heated water seeks to rise just like hot air over a campfire. Eventually it finds a place where there is a crack or other natural opening, bubbles out of the ground, and we have a hot springs! During its stay underground, sometimes under intense heat, the water absorbs minerals and colors from the surrounding rocks. There is often a diverse array of chemicals that serve as a telltale history of the water's underground journey. If the water filtered through limestone, for example, it will carry dissolved calcium compounds. Sulfur, copper, iron, sodium, and phosphorous are commonly found minerals and metals that mix with the water, often to the delight of bathers who value the mineral waters as healthful.

The happily bubbling little springs of water may percolate like a natural coffee pot or may gush hundreds of gallons of water under pressure (artesian) from gravity, or it may just burst forth in periodic geysers when enough water has filled some complicated subterranean plumbing maze to its boil-over point, spouting steam and scalding water. A sudden earthquake can shift a fault and alter the flow of a springs or close it off completely! A visit to Yellowstone National Park in Wyoming or Montana will reveal an amazing array of geothermal activity. Yellowstone is the world's fair of hot springs.

Some of the hot water from a typical springs will soak back into the ground, some will evaporate, and some will flow into a nearby stream and end up in the ocean, where the whole process can begin again. That's why a hot spring can bubble along contentedly for centuries, and the flow of minerals in the water will leave a mound of accumulated buildup as evidence of its longevity.

One other kind of hot springs is referenced in this book, and although its origins are not as natural as geothermal groundwater that has risen to the surface, it is nonetheless a common source of soaking water for bathers in Colorado. Wells are drilled in the right place, either intentionally or accidentally,

Geology of Hot Springs

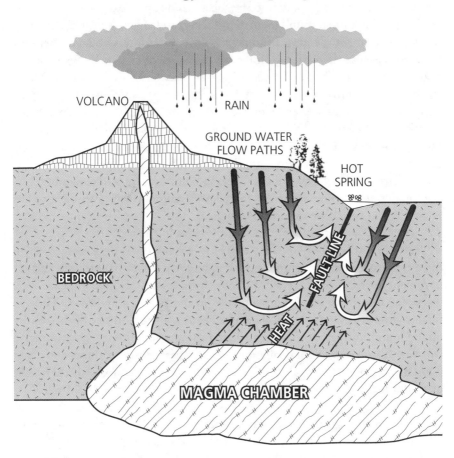

tapping into heated groundwater. Some hot-water wells are remnants of oil drilling that annoyed the drillers when the wells spouted hot water instead of the oil they hoped for. There are several of these in southeast central Colorado, and they can be more than a thousand feet deep. Some wells are drilled into known geothermal zones with the express intention of tapping the hot water. The southwest-central area of the state has some of those. No matter how the water gets to the surface, it has been warmed by its proximity to magma pockets and has absorbed minerals and colors during its stay beneath the surface. See the diagram above.

Would it surprise you to learn that there are many, many hot springs that will probably never be the pleasure of the hot-potting crowd? They are underwater on the ocean floor! Just as there are mountain ranges under the ocean waters, so there are convection currents of underground hot water that percolate their way into the cool water of the ocean depths. There are steam vents and hot-water vents that support exotic life forms unique to the subsea world of hot springs. Something else you might want to consider as you parboil delightedly in some remote mountain hot springs, is the fact that the underground network of cracks and rivers and pools of water is often quite large. Although we have yet to develop reliable ways to "see" underground (regrettably, say the oil drillers), we know some of the reservoirs of water that supply hot springs are relatively unaffected by drought or particularly heavy seasonal rainfall. This means the rain that fell last week up the hill is probably not the same stuff gurgling about your feet. In fact, you might find it amusing to consider that the water surrounding you could be made up of some of the very same raindrops that plopped on the head of Kit Carson more than a century ago, or a Ute Indian warrior living two hundred years before that. Certainly most of the hot springs of Colorado were well known to native peoples centuries before the current crop of soakers came along. That's just part of the hot springs mystique.

One other introductory thought, and it has to do with culture, too. Throughout the last 10,000 years, humans have enjoyed nature's hot-water wonders. There have been cultures that have held very high religious and social esteem for geothermal waters. The ancient baths of Greece and Italy were hallmarks of society, especially since indoor plumbing and automated temperature control as we know them today were yet to be developed. Most of Europe and the Orient have a legacy of spiritual and social custom that recognized the benefits of hot springs. Here on our own continent, native peoples attributed great healing powers and spiritual significance to the mineral water flows. In Colorado, the prevalent Ute and Arapaho tribes held hot springs sites in reverence and often fought wars (a distinctly human thing to do) over the right to indulge in them. It would be good for all of us to enjoy the hot springs of Colorado with tolerance toward others while we remember that civilizations past and present have all had their unique ways of "taking the waters."

ETHICS AND ETIQUETTE

It is always good to remember that whatever hot springs you enjoy is a shared resource. Treat the site and those who share it with respect and thoughtfulness. Whether the hot springs is a public or a private facility, there are essential, fundamental rules of conduct that simply preclude inconsiderate actions like littering or drunken, rowdy behavior. Don't make a nuisance of yourself by leaving cans, paper, or bottles behind. Most commercial establishments have an inviolable rule prohibiting alcoholic beverages, if not to prevent foolishness on the part of patrons, then as a liability measure.

There's a hot springs in Montana where a sign at the pool entrance reminds you that they do not swim in your toilet and prefer that you not piddle in their pool. That seems simple enough. Never urinate into a pool. That may sound obvious, but the health and courtesy issues may need to be explained to youngsters. Be careful with human and pet waste disposal when visiting remote locations. Could there be anything more repugnant than having that sort of thing intrude on an otherwise healthy and relaxing visit to a backcountry springs?

Respecting private property is an essential rule to observe. If you see a no-trespassing sign, then stay out. Stay on designated routes and don't thrash around in the mud with your ATV, making a mess of the roads or trails. What would you think if somebody did that stuff on *your* land? Acting responsibly means hot springs will be kept open to the public instead of being closed due to overuse and abuse. Try to leave a location in better condition than you found it.

Another chapter in the etiquette handbook deals with intruding on someone who is using a pool ahead of you. Now, this clearly is a matter where common sense applies, because it is not expected that you would defer "ownership" of a public hot springs pool that is intended to be shared by many individuals. If the first person into Glenwood Hot Springs "owned" the pool, the real owners would promptly be out of business. On the other hand, if you have hiked into an isolated hot pot with a squadron of kids and find it already occupied, it is simply good manners to give the courtesy of leaving it to them, or at the very least asking if they would mind your company. Many locations have multiple soaking pools and you can find one for yourself, but in any case, a simple question will let you know. You will find that gesture appreciated by others, and by you yourself when you have your solitude interrupted by unexpected visitors. In my experience, most often you will be invited to join in if the pool is big enough, or at least be advised that you can have it to yourself in a short while. Use good judgment and simply ask yourself how you would like to be treated if you were in the other person's position. That rule of conduct is especially important where clothing-optional standards are in effect.

NATURISM

The world of hot springs and those who fancy them is unique and diverse. There are legions of staunch followers who might qualify as a cult when measured by their reverence. Then again, there are those who drop in on a hot pot now and then but really do not go out of their way much in pursuit of new waters. Among the more ardent followers, there are distinct subcultures whose guiding influences are specific enough to mention. For example, I have encountered people whose mission is to soak daily in mineral waters as a contribution toward their good health. While it has never really been proven by solid scientific evidence, there is a long history of testimony extolling the benefits of preventing and curing diseases by bathing in mineral water. Some aficionados enjoy the revelation of free-spiritedness that seems to be a big part of the hot-pot scene. And some of us simply seek out the springs because there is almost nothing more relaxing than a good long soak in nature's own hot water.

If you are new to the world of hot springs, you may be surprised at how many of them have a clothing-optional standard. *Clothing-optional* is a euphemism of sorts; in simple terms it means you may bathe nude. Skinny-dipping has a daring, renegade connotation that is not quite the same as clothing-optional. *Naturism* is the latest term applying to an outlook that advocates a natural, unfettered way of doing things. A *naturist* is one who appreciates things the way nature created them. This includes valuing things like environmental sensitivity, a less-cluttered lifestyle, and of course, soaking in a hot tub without any clothes on, because wearing bathing attire is viewed as pretentious and goes against the natural and simple way of things. Naturism is considered by its adherents to be healthful, sensible, simple, and quite devoid of sexual connotations.

Hot springs that have a clothing-optional provision are not all set aside for naturists, but are usually very explicit about separating sexuality from soaking without a swimsuit. This is not nudism, but might better be thought of as tolerance toward the view that you can shed the pretense of contrived social rules right along with your bathing suit. It is uncanny how social posturing seems to fade and everyone becomes equal when they're naked. The social distinctions between a schoolteacher, a federal judge, and a bartender quickly blur. If you have conservative tendencies like I do, it will take some adjustments before you are completely comfortable slipping into the pool buck naked, but it is also something that soon seems quite normal and, well, pretty natural.

If the whole idea of clothing-optional soaking seems frightening and impossible for you, I suggest you either avoid places which permit (or proclaim) naturist views or acquaint yourself with the idea under more private conditions. Remember that clothing-optional means just that—they are *optional*. That's not the same as a mandate to be in the buff under all circumstances. Most hot springs with a naturist outlook will welcome you with whatever you want to wear, and your feelings of self-consciousness will be more from your imagination than from any contempt or scorn from fellow soakers. You might slip into the pool and doff your duds under cover of the water. Still, if you want to break into the clothing-optional culture gently, perhaps the best opportunity would be to visit one of the remote locations when nobody else is around! Just remember that clothing-optional is quite the norm in isolated locations. If you blush when you take a shower at home, my advice is to stick to the public pools where suits are required.

How to Use This Book

ORGANIZATION

This book is organized by geographic structure. Colorado, being generally square in shape, was easy for me to somewhat arbitrarily divide into four quadrants. The northeast, northwest, southeast, and southwest regions all have their respective hot springs and display an abbreviated indication as the first part of each site description. For example, SW 1 is an abbreviation for southwest number 1. The numbers are a bit arbitrary also, and simply serve to help you find the springs easily when navigating the book sequentially. In other words, if you are looking in the back at an appendix cross-reference list of family pools, it may refer to SW 4 along with the name Orvis Hot Springs. Then you can page back to the section on southwest locations, and you will immediately know that

you need to turn ahead a few more pages if you see SW 1 before you. It's a logical arrangement, once you know how it works.

Geographically, most of the thermal activity is in the western half of Colorado, and the southwestern zone is clearly blessed with the most springs. Keep in mind, though, that this is not intended to be an exhaustive guide to all hot springs in Colorado. Not every geothermal site is deemed suitable for bathing, and some are simply off-limits because they are restricted private property (later in the book I list a few of these places for your reference). It is my desire to include in this book the hot springs that are appropriate for a wide audience, so an algae-choked swamp full of snakes and bugs would not make the list, even if technically it is a hot springs. You can find an exhaustive list of even the most minute thermal indications using Colorado Geological Survey publications, if that is your desire; they are listed in the back of the book. If you are like most people, however, you probably would choose a soaking spot you could get to without risk of being shot for trespassing, or one you could hike to without needing to use technical climbing gear. In fact, you may be most interested in hot springs you can drive to easily.

Organizationally, each chapter will have a general description of the hot springs and enough information outlined on the first page so that you can get a good idea of what the site is about in a few moments of reading. I will assume a rudimentary set of navigational skills on your part, meaning that you know which way is north and that you can read a simple map. Each section has brief comments about the best time of year to visit and the services available, but remember that there is some subjectivity involved when I suggest that summers may be too hot or that in winter a site is a fine apres ski destination. The reference to available services generally means full services like restaurants, fuel, hospitals, and motels. There may be some closer location that has a gasoline pump, but those are variable enough that I simply will point you to the nearest place where you can go if your car breaks down or if you need a treatment for snakebite.

USING THE MAPS AND DIRECTIONS

In each section describing a hot springs, I include a paragraph on finding the springs and a reference to maps. Here again I assume some fundamental navigating skills, but I believe that with a Colorado highway map and the maps and directions provided in this book, you will have no trouble finding the sites. The quadrangle maps I specify are U.S. Geological Survey topographical maps that are available directly from the USGS (address in Appendix B), or at local sporting goods, climbing, or specialty outdoor sports stores. For locations that are somewhat remote, I strongly suggest the USGS quadrangles and a national forest map (addresses also in Appendix B). The highway map will get you close, and the simple maps and descriptions in this book should get you the rest of the way if you pay attention.

For those readers progressive enough to carry a handheld GPS receiver, I have included the GPS coordinates. I admit to being something of a techno-geek myself, and have used a GPS unit for many years on hunting trips locally and outside this country. They represent simply amazing technology that has become affordable for nearly everyone, but you still will need to know how to use a map and compass sometimes, and being able to read directions is a handy thing too. Having a handheld GPS receiver can get you home in the dark or during a blinding snowstorm, as long as your batteries hold up.

PRECAUTIONS AND PLANNING

As with any trip to an unknown area, you should plan ahead. That means you should take some simple precautions, like letting someone know where you are going and when you expect to return. Taking maps with you is always a good idea. I would be embarrassed to admit how many times I have gone on a wilderness adventure with my horses and left my map at home on the kitchen table!

Check with local land-management agencies like the USDA Forest Service to be sure trails are open or that a road has not been washed out by a spring flood.

If you are headed to a hot springs that is somewhat remote, be sure you have all the emergency gear you need in your backpack or in your vehicle. Things like a first-aid kit, water, matches, and spare clothing should be where you can easily get at them. If you are driving, make sure your car has a spare, your fluid levels are all safe, and that you carry some tools if you have any idea how to use them. Keep flares, extra blankets, and water for that suddenly leaky radiator. Oh, yes—make sure your fuel gauge is accurate!

I will not try to create a list here for every circumstance, but use common sense, think ahead to what could go wrong, and be prepared. Perhaps being prepared means no more than calling ahead to the hot-springs resort where you are headed to see if they are open and what their hours of business are. In the back of the book (in Appendix B) I have provided a list of phone and fax numbers, street addresses, and even e-mail and website addresses, if resort operators are progressive enough to have them. Once again, it pays to plan ahead.

DETAILS AND AREA HIGHLIGHTS

For each site discussed in the book, the overview section will describe the springs in greater detail and provide occasional historical insights. I personally find the history fascinating, not only for the perspective it adds but also because it enhances my enjoyment of the journey to the hot springs. There is much more to be told, of course, but this is a guidebook for hot springs and not a history text, so I have restrained myself as best I can.

Throughout the book I provide descriptions—not only of temperatures and dimensions so that you know what to expect of a springs physically, but, more importantly, I have tried to describe the "feel" of each site. There are many hot springs scattered across the state of Colorado, each unique and appealing in its own way. I hope to have captured some sense of the attitude and personality each one projects. This is a subjective portrayal. I may find public nudity mildly disconcerting, while you as the reader may laugh at my silly, conservative ways and feel quite comfortable in naturist environs.

One more thing you will discover at the end of a site description is an "Area highlights" section. Colorado is a vacation paradise, and there are simply endless opportunities for recreation. I assume most people who use this guidebook will do more than just make a beeline for the springs, jump in, and then bolt for home without a wasted second. Toward that end I have tried to give the reader an array of local attractions to consider as a natural complement to the hot-springs experience. Career hot-potters may use the springs as a launch pad to other adventures, and family vacations can be centered within a cluster of geographically convenient springs. At the end of a given section I hope you will feel that you simply have more options than time.

RESOURCES

Within this book are numerous resources to help you enjoy finding and soaking in Colorado's best hot springs. In addition to the individual listings of hot springs, two appendices are located in the back of the book. Appendix A groups hot springs by nongeographic selection criteria. For example, there is a list of clothing-optional locations in case that is your primary consideration for visiting hot springs. Appendix B has all of the necessary addresses and phone numbers, along with e-mail addresses and even some websites and fax numbers. You will also find the addresses and phone numbers for some of the relevant public agencies where you can purchase maps, get current data on area road closures, or obtain tourist information—such as state parks and campgrounds.

With the explosion of information available on the internet, it is no surprise that many of the hot springs have their own web pages. Those of you familiar with searching the internet may need no help finding out more about Colorado's resources, but for your convenience there is a "starter kit" of web addresses to point you in the right direction.

HOT SPOTS AND NOT SPOTS

NOT INCLUDED

Earlier in the book I mentioned that this is not an exhaustive source describing every geothermal water site in Colorado. That is not so much a disclaimer as a clarification. This volume is intended to be a guidebook to the best of what Colorado offers that also is open to you, the public. It would be irresponsible for me to tell you about a great hot-springs pool that happens to be on posted private property that is protected by an armed guard who has explicit directions to shoot first and ask questions later. I once visited a place that made me wonder if the guard's gun was loaded or just for show, but rest assured, that spring is not listed in this book.

There are several hot springs on posted (No Trespassing) private property. The publisher of this book and your author do not wish to be defendants in a lawsuit because we published the location of a hot springs whose owners do not want troops of hikers or motor-home convoys showing up without an invitation.

A great spot that won't make the book.

A great spot known to locals as Walden Pond on the eastern edge of the Mount Zirkel Wilderness is just such a place. It is a beautiful location and a wonderful spring, but simply cannot be included because it is on private property. Juniper Hot Springs on the Yampa River, Antelope Warm Springs, and Cebolla Hot Springs are examples of what were once developed springs that are now generally in disrepair and unused; they are clearly posted no trespassing. Rico Hot Springs is posted, also, and even if you could get there without risking trouble, it is too laden with heavy metals, minerals, and unpleasant fumes to enjoy.

Another category for de-listing includes springs like Pinkerton Hot Springs and Penny Hot Springs. They are right next to the highway now, after roadway improvements, and not my idea of great places to go soaking, even if it were possible. Penny Hot Springs is just down the road from Redstone and is used by some diehards ignoring the rush of cars just above their heads, but I would rather not send you there. There are locations like Piedra Hot Springs that have measurably deteriorated, leaving me to question their sanitation; they also do not qualify for this book. I would be remiss to include places just for the sake of completeness and have you wonder what state of mind induced me to direct you there. Though the condition of a given spring may change with time, for better or worse, I will not send you someplace I found questionable. The references I have provided in the appendices may guide the intrepid to their own conclusions if they choose to explore beyond what I have recommended.

In summary, though there are several hot springs that are legitimate sources of hot water from the earth, I am including only those that I feel are appropriate for a guidebook of this type. There is an exciting abundance of beautiful and historic hot springs in the state of Colorado. Enjoy "taking her waters."

AUTHOR'S FAVORITES

Picking my favorite hot springs is a daunting challenge when I consider the variety and beauty of what Colorado offers. There are secret hideaways, wilderness hot spots, and lavish public spas. You can soak in historic locations, friendly community pools, and pampering places that rival some of the finest in America. The following listings are designed to help you visit the type (or types) of hot springs that you prefer. Being included on my list simply means that these springs are my personal favorites among a stellar group of candidates. Among all the hot springs across this vast state, I can count on one hand the number of sites to which I would be reluctant to send my own mother. That should tell you how good most of them are. The best thing to do is visit as many as you can and draw your own conclusions about your favorite places. Is that like making it your mission to try every flavor down at the ice-cream store?

Best Secluded-Experience Locations

The concept of a secluded experience is difficult to quantify. What is secluded to you might seem like a New York City sidewalk at lunchtime to me. Complicating matters even more are considerations such as the best time of year to visit the sites, and private springs versus public springs. Still, all things being equal, this is an easy choice for me. Conundrum Hot Springs is without a doubt my favorite hot springs in the entire state of Colorado. Its basic remoteness and the relative difficulty of getting there guarantee some solitude, and when you arrive you will revel in the knowledge that this is what a natural hot springs is supposed to be. Located in the scenic Maroon Bells–Snowmass Wilderness just outside of Aspen, it features a stunning setting and a superb soak.

Following in the runner-up position is Rainbow Hot Springs in the beautiful Weminuche Wilderness. Here again, you eliminate many intruders because you must walk in to find it. The springs is in a picturesque setting adjacent to the west fork of the San Juan River, and the hike itself provides great scenery. When I was there last on a gorgeous, sunny day in early July, I had the place completely to myself, although I would not expect you to find such exclusivity for your soak in nature's wilderness theater often.

Best Family Locations

Choosing the best family location is difficult, again due to differing ideas about what makes an ideal family spot, but I am confident that my choices will leave your entire family delighted. Without peer in Colorado, and probably most of the West, Glenwood Hot Springs is simply the best. Bigger is not always better, but in this case the sheer size and scope of the facilities virtually guarantee a thrill for everyone. Superbly done and with a host of conveniences, amusements, and features, you will not leave without promising yourself to return. It really is that good.

Following close on the heels of Glenwood Hot Springs is Ouray Hot Springs. It makes me grin just to think about the place. In what may be one of Colorado's most charismatic towns, because of its location and the "feel" of the community, Ouray Hot Springs is versatile, big enough to lose a busload of kids in, and it will most certainly put a smile on your face the whole time you are there.

A consideration I used to determine what makes an ideal family location is the *proximity factor*. Candidates for this category needed to provide a wide variety of things to do besides playing in the hot springs. Although I have never known a child who tired quickly of splashing around a swimming pool, it is good to have lots to choose from any time of year, just for the sake of variety. You can ski, skate, fish, hike, float, visit historic sites, and do a bazillion other things until the cows come home. When you read the sections on Glenwood and Ouray hot springs, you will see in the "Area Highlights" why they meet this criterion so well. You and your family need never be bored.

It is important to the discussion on ideal family locations to consider community pools. These are hot springs-fed pools that are the focal point, help define, and are woven into the very fabric of the town. Almost by definition, the community is small, and that is part of what makes the pool so important. Everybody in town knows about it, all the kids learn to swim there, and several generations probably have grown up using the springs. Certainly Glenwood Hot Springs and Ouray Hot Springs meet those requirements, but special mention must also be made of Splashland Pool, Salida Hot Springs, and Trimble Hot Springs—all are sterling examples of what defines the town pool. In a community-centric pool, do not be surprised when the owners and lifeguards can call most of the swimmers by name. These are places you can be proud of and feel safe taking your child to learn to swim. When all is said and done, that may be the best possible use for a hot springs.

Best Clothing-Optional Locations

This is a subjective category, perhaps even more than the others I have mentioned. To be considered for the clothing-optional list, obviously a hot springs location would have to tolerate and even endorse clothing-optional standards. More than just naturist leanings are required for inclusion as a top choice, though, since there are many springs in Colorado where soaking in the buff is well accepted. The ideal clothing-optional hot springs must make that comfortable even for someone who is still new to the cadre of skinny-buffers, in addition to providing a great soak. Only a few can do that.

At the top of the list of great places to slip into nothing and slip into the pool is Valley View Hot Springs. Idyllic, relaxing, and immensely charming, this is a place that will make you feel like you were a stuffy old coot before you tried it, and, if you already count yourself part of the clothing-optional society, you'll feel that you've come home again. Located in the high-elevation San Luis Valley, and enjoying great vistas, Valley View Hot Springs is a retreat and a revelation that promises to unclutter your view of the world.

The Desert Reef Beach Club is an anomaly of sorts, much like any oasis in the desert might be. Slightly counter-culture, addictively relaxing, and possessed of fine character in a humble sort of way, it is a semiprivate hot springs that enjoys a very staunch following. Surprisingly close to large population centers including the Denver metro area, Colorado Springs, and Pueblo, it is at once both convenient and hard to find, with an exclusive flavor. Low-key and unassuming, it has an uncanny way of making clothing-optional rules seem very normal.

Best Character and Personality Locations

When you walk away from a place and find yourself saying, "Wow, that place is really, really cool," then you know you've been to a hot springs with character and personality. It's the kind of spot you can't wait to tell your closest friends about, and that you know you will go back to visit if you are ever anywhere near it again. Although most of the hot springs in Colorado are wonderful and make me want to revisit them, to make this short list takes something special that is tough to quantify.

Ask people who have been there and they likely will agree that Strawberry Park Hot Springs, just north of Steamboat Springs, is a great place, and they will be smiling when they tell you. It's almost as if everyone who goes there has some special memory from past visits. Maybe it is the mountain setting, the handsome rockwork, or perhaps the lovely stream tumbling through the middle

Conundrum Hot Springs.

of the little valley, but probably it is the combination of them all that makes this a sweet spot. Off the beaten tourist path, a family playground by day and clothing-optional by night, it is a place that will draw you back again and again.

Is it fair to have one hot springs be included in two "Best" lists? There will be little to question when you finally visit Conundrum Hot Springs. Almost as hard to leave as to get to, you will be in relatively select company at this hot springs. The pools are small, sparkling jewels of crystalline water in a setting that can only be described as spectacular. It is not only the setting but also the journey that makes this a place you will likely list among your favorites. You must earn your passage to this one, but that is part of its charm. When God created hot springs, surely this was the model.

Northwest Colorado Hot Springs

NW 1

Steamboat Springs Health and Recreation Association

General description: Modern, well-appointed health club and hot springs pools.

Location: In the northwest, 40 miles east of Craig and 160 miles west of Fort Collins.

Development: Fully equipped health club facilities, and swimming and soaking pools.

Best time to visit: Year-round resort, but summer and winter are great choices.

Restrictions: None.

Access: Easy and convenient year-round access by public roads.

Water temperature: Moderate, varying from 82 to 102 degrees F.

Services: Full services are available in Steamboat Springs.

Camping: None. Summer campgrounds nearby.

Maps: Steamboat Springs Quadrangle; Routt National Forest; Arapaho National Forest.

GPS coordinates: N 40 28 58 W 106 49 37

Finding the springs: From Craig, in the northwest part of the state, drive east on U.S. Highway 40 for just less than one hour to Steamboat Springs. From Denver, take Interstate 70 west to Colorado Highway 9 at Silverthorn and turn north toward Kremmling. Continue north on US 40 to Steamboat Springs. In Steamboat Springs, US 40 is known as Lincoln Avenue. The Health and Recreation Association is easily visible on the north side of the road, at 136 Lincoln Avenue.

Overview: Steamboat Springs may epitomize the best of Colorado, in that it has managed to retain its historic character and personality in a frenzied world while offering enough of the amenities of civilization to stay abreast of the twenty-first century. Named in the early 1800s by French trappers who heard a hollow, resonant "chugging" sound, they assumed that their long days afield had ended with the discovery of a steamboat on the Yampa River. The sound was produced, not by a steamboat engine, but by a small underground chamber

Steamboat Springs Health and
Recreation Association, Strawberry Hot Springs

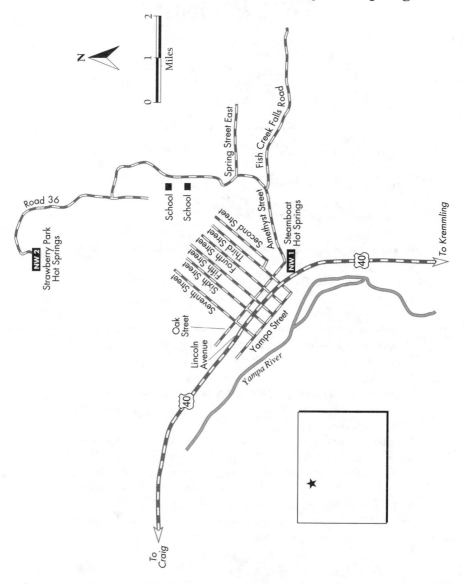

of compressed steam and hot water that regularly urped its noisy release. The name stuck, even after blasting for the railroad in 1908 altered subsurface structure enough to "unchug" the previously rhythmic sound of the springs. Steamboat Springs is the social and historic center of an area that boasts 150 hot springs sprinkled from river to field. Of them all, Heart Spring, which feeds the Steamboat Springs Health and Recreation Association (SSHRA), is the only one developed for commercial hot bathing.

Heart Spring was discovered in 1874 by James Crawford, the first European settler to use the springs, although the Yampatika Ute Indians had appreciated and fought for the area's hot water sources for centuries. The Utes and Arapahos are said to have had fierce battles for dominion over the sacred grounds, believing them to be a source of physical and spiritual healing. The SSHRA reports that the last significant battle between these longtime enemies was staged on the hill just behind what is now the club's beautiful pool complex. In 1884 Crawford helped build a log bathhouse over the springs, where to date there have been several transformations of the site: a pit in the dirt was followed by a log structure, a stone building, and now a bathhouse of concrete and river stone. This is the source of the 102 degree F water that supplies the heart-shaped pool as well as the remaining hot spas and an Olympic-size swimming pool. Heart Spring was given its name in 1931 by H. W. Gossard, the last man to own it before SSHRA bought the property. He was among the many who improved the facilities with bigger and newer construction. Gossard also added the now-traditional winter carnival to the town's lineup of activities.

The Steamboat Springs Health and Recreation Association has a wide range of attractions to recommend it besides the huge, 82-degree F swimming pool and cozy soaking spas, which vary from 98 to 102 degrees. The extensive landscaping that surrounds the pool is beautiful, and often is done by locals

Steamboat Hot Springs has classy pools and a great facility.

who trade their work for membership privileges. There is a water slide into its own pool that beckons the child in all of us. Weight-lifting and workout facilities, tennis courts, aerobic and cardio centers, saunas, massages, and a snack bar all add to your enjoyment of the hot springs. You can even rent a swimsuit or towel and use the child-care services while you're getting your exercise or sunning on the decks outside.

The seven hot springs near the pools at SSHRA also make for a delightful walking tour of the immediate area. Self-guided tour brochures of the area are available at SSHRA and the chamber of commerce.

Plan to take a couple of hours to walk the 2 miles, starting at the health club. Walking west along Lincoln Avenue to Iron Spring, you can see the ferrous water that once was the elixir of choice for Iron Water Lemonade. Soda Spring now has a gazebo that marks the demise of the effervescent springs, a victim of highway construction. Hoof prints around Sulphur Spring–fed Sweetwater Lake suggest that it may be more popular with native wildlife than with humans—who often find the pungent sulfur smell objectionable. Curiously, the Indians also thought the odor was a measure of curative ability and sought its benefits.

The original Steamboat Spring and nearby Black Sulphur Spring are across the Yampa River. Black Sulphur's appearance is a result of the natural chemical reactions in the water. Consulting your guide map, you will discover Lithia Spring and its milky, lithium-laden waters. Although heralded as a treatment for manic-depressive disorders, the actual lithium content of the water probably is not high enough to qualify for that purpose, and you are discouraged from drinking any of the untreated waters from these springs. The last stop on your walking tour is Sulphur Cave, with its legends of spiritual influence. The Native Americans reportedly found vision and strength in the vapors, but perhaps the ancient mycelial fungus (the same form dating back four billion years) and interesting formations will seem more appealing to you.

All in all, the springs of Steamboat Springs are varied and fascinating, both in terms of their history and their geology. Certainly you can reflect on an amazing legacy while you soak in the same waters over which love and war have been made.

Area highlights: For a town as small as Steamboat Springs, there is an amazing array of activities to keep you busy and entertained. Like much of this beautiful state, there are seemingly endless recreational opportunities. You can float, fish, or kayak the Yampa River, which flows through town and features a kayaking slalom course just across from the SSHRA. Sail or angle in Stagecoach Reservoir, Lake Catamount, or Steamboat Lake.

The Mount Zirkel and Flat Tops wilderness areas are superb for hiking, scenery, camping, and rock climbing. In town you can rock climb indoors, see a rodeo in summer, roller skate, or take a tour of the Steamboat Ski Area. Maybe you will find your pleasure in renting a kayak, canoe, or inner tube for the river; or perhaps a mountain bike, ATV, or horse will provide the adventure you desire. There also are hot air balloon festivals, cowboy rodeo roundups, motorcycle races, music festivals, brewfests, and golf courses. In winter, if you are an alpine skier, snowmobiler, or snowshoe hiker, you will find plenty of snow and beautiful terrain. You will run out of time and energy before you deplete the list of recreations and adventures to be had in the Steamboat Springs area.

NW 2

Strawberry Park Hot Springs

(See map on page 18)

General description: Secluded mountain setting with nicely developed pools.
Location: In northwest Colorado, just north of Steamboat Springs.
Development: Nicely developed native stone soaking pools next to creek.
Best times to visit: Summer and early fall provide the best access.
Restrictions: None during daylight. Adults only after dark.
Access: Fair access. Road is moderately steep dirt for last half of route. Access will be difficult without a four-wheel-drive vehicle in winter and during muddy spring thaw.
Water temperature: Moderate and variable from 100 to 105 degrees F.
Services: Nearest full services are in Steamboat Springs. Some rustic cabins are available.
Camping: None.
Maps: Rocky Peak Quadrangle; Routt National Forest.
GPS coordinates: N 40 33 34 W 106 51 00
Finding the springs: U.S. Highway 40 runs through the town of Steamboat Springs as Lincoln Avenue, and you must turn north just west of Steamboat Springs Health and Recreation Association, following the signs for Fish Creek Falls Road and the hospital. From Fish Creek Falls Road, drive about a third of a mile to Amethyst Road on your left (heading west), take Amethyst Road through a rural residential area for 3.2 miles before the pavement ends. Drive another 3.2 miles on a dirt road that is sometimes steep and may require a four-wheel-drive vehicle in winter or during muddy conditions. Keep driving, even though you suspect you will end up in the wilderness. Strawberry Park is at the end of the road.

Overview: This is a beautifully picturesque hot springs with a colorful history and is one of the most pleasant rural settings in Colorado. Owned at one time by the city of Steamboat Springs, it became an administrative nuisance because of the bawdy crowds that frequented the springs. The locals spin yarns about wild parties involving copious amounts of intoxicants and mattresses strewn about in a haphazard commune. Images of Woodstock and a less-inhibited generation are easy to conjure upon hearing the colorful stories. Still, the springs are delightfully enticing, and the interesting history only adds to its charm.

Long ago Strawberry Park might have been remote enough to escape too much scrutiny, and the imagined debauchery may well have exceeded the reality, but encroaching development and a growing population in the area eventually made it more visible. In 1981 the city divested itself of the springs on the heels of a drunken brawl where a few too many got hurt and made a spectacle too embarrassing for the comfort of a town increasingly concerned with its image. Ownership of the hot springs passed to local resident Don Johnson, who has made the area something of a lifetime project with delightfully integrated stonework and handsomely rustic buildings. The new ownership and charging usage fees reduced the social flavor from wild to progressive. After dark, attendance is restricted to those at least 18 years old, and a free-spirited ambiance encourages leaving your swimsuit on the deck. While you may be in

Strawberry Hot Springs, an accessible mountain hideaway.

the minority by wearing your swim togs, you will probably not be scorned.

The setting is beautifully remote while still being accessible, and your view of the Colorado sky will be enhanced by the roar of the stream tumbling through the middle of the park and the smell of the surrounding fir trees. The water has no chemicals added and is a very comfortable temperature, and if necessary, you can easily find a temperature more to your liking simply by moving closer to or away from the inlet of hot water tumbling down the hill. You can even pamper yourself with massage services, which are available on-site. The entire facility can be rented for private functions and it frequently is enlivened by busloads of children on field trips from nearby schools. Charming, romantically rustic, and nicely appointed, this is one of the prettiest of northwest Colorado's hot springs.

Area highlights: The area near Strawberry Park Hot Springs is a recreational paradise. Besides being close to Steamboat Hot Springs with its summer-long list of music festivals, car and motorcycle weeks, rodeos, and brewfests, the nearby Yampa River provides floating and fishing opportunities, and even has a kayak race course for the whitewater folks. Steamboat Ski Area has its lower runs virtually in town, and features a vertical drop of 3,600 feet. Also close at hand are the Mount Zirkel and Flat Tops wilderness areas if you prefer smaller crowds, and there are hunting, fishing, hiking, and sightseeing opportunities in the adjacent Routt National Forest. Steamboat Lake, Lake Catamount, and Stagecoach Reservoir are conveniently close by if you like to sail, wet a line, or water ski.

The cultural and outdoor recreational opportunities are as varied as they are exciting.

NW 3

Hot Sulphur Springs

General description: Newly renovated vacation spa in an isolated community.
Location: Between Steamboat Springs and Denver on U.S. Highway 40.
Development: Pools, soaking caves, and a small conference facility.
Best time to visit: Summer is probably the best season to visit.
Restrictions: None.
Access: Easy and convenient year-round access by public roads.
Water temperature: Moderate and variable from 102 to 108 degrees F.
Services: The small town of Hot Sulphur Springs has essential services—gas, food, etc.
Camping: None.
Maps: Hot Sulphur Springs Quadrangle; Arapaho National Forest.
GPS coordinates: N 40 04 29 W 106 06 40.
Finding the springs: From Steamboat Springs, drive southeast on US 40 about 45 minutes to Hot Sulphur Springs. From Denver, drive west on Interstate 70 about a half hour and take US 40 north at Idaho Springs for an hour up to Hot Sulphur Springs.

The actual resort is on the west side of tiny Hot Sulphur Springs, just across the Colorado River. From the middle of town take any street a block north and catch Grand Street, driving west across the bridge over the river. You can see the hot springs from US 40.

Overview: Under the ownership of only a few people since the Ute Indians frequented the springs long ago, it has only recently been renovated and made into a year-round facility.

According to the facility's manager, Susan Thurston, the man who originally developed the springs was the wealthy and influential publisher of the Denver newspaper, the *Rocky Mountain News*. The spa now features an assortment of pools and soaking tubs that have made Hot Sulphur Springs a friendly, versatile place to take a business retreat or a family vacation. Besides the usual swimming pools, soaking tubs, and massage treatments, there is a modest conference room, allowing the facility to be used as a very relaxing business escape. How can you feel anything but cooperative and devoid of aggression after spending the day soaking, sunning, and having your tensions massaged into oblivion? Perhaps the Strategic Arms Limitations negotiations should be held at Hot Sulphur Springs!

Outside there is a small pool and a larger, kidney-shaped pool with generous sunning decks and nicely landscaped grounds. Enjoying a flow of about

Hot Sulphur Springs

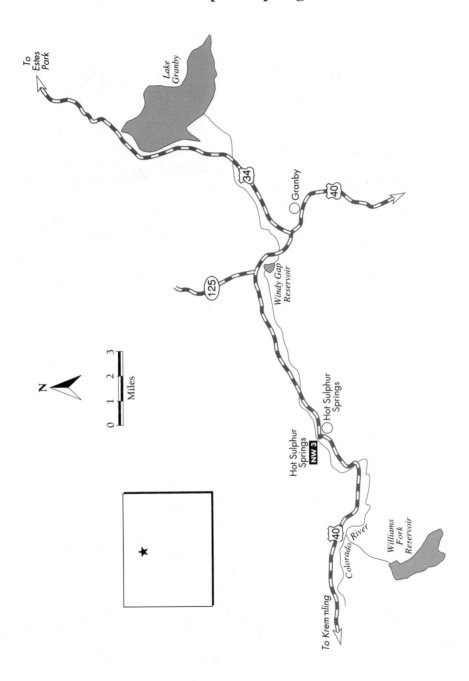

Freshly remodeled Hot Sulphur Springs.

5,000 gallons per hour, the springs feed the Ute Pool in back, which has a unique spillway and water entering at almost 118 degrees F, and also a jet pool. Inside there are small private baths for individual relaxation. You may decide to enjoy a massage, a facial, or perhaps just relax in the post-massage lounge in a towel wrap. There are separate, segregated vapor caves that rent by the hour, and a health-food snack bar to replenish your energies.

Since the days in the nineteenth century when William Byers wrestled with the Indians for legal ownership of the springs, Byers's heirs and the family of James Dougherty, who bought the site from Byers in 1943, have mostly kept Hot Sulphur Springs as a summer resort. At one time there were grand dreams of an international vacation lodge for business people and others of stature, like the site's developer. Byers built a four-story hotel (which burned in 1903), a racetrack, a covered pool, and his own summer home on the site. But getting there was difficult until the Denver and Rio Grande Railroad arrived in 1928 and provided the convenient access that might have fueled Byers's dreams. Access through Moffat Tunnel brought changes to the area, but somehow Hot Sulphur Springs never grew into the high-profile destination it was envisioned to be.

Still somewhat isolated in its high mountain home surrounded by the Arapaho National Forest and bordered by the famous Colorado River, it is only now beginning to see the recognition that will raise its visibility. There have been notables since William Byers to visit the Hot Sulphur Springs, of course. Author Zane Grey and river-runner John Wesley Powell, for example, as well as a host of local outlaws and officials, have absorbed the therapy of these sometimes sulfurous waters over the years. Regardless of the public notoriety of its visitors, perhaps the most valuable and lasting recommendation for this resort on the edge of the river is its setting. With views of the impressive Longs Peak (elevation 14,255 feet) and access to Rocky Mountain National Park, Hot Sulphur Springs will refresh your mind, your spirit, and your body.

Area highlights: With seemingly endless views of the Arapaho National Forest, a world-class river that runs from just out in front of your pool all the way to Mexico, and some of Colorado's most beautiful high mountains, this is a marvelous place to begin some wonderful outdoor adventures. The headwaters of the Colorado River are just to the north in the Never Summer Mountains Wilderness Area, but you can enjoy the Indian Peaks, Neota, and Commanche Peak wilderness areas nearby too. Rocky Mountain National Park, and Roosevelt and Routt national forests offer fishing, hiking, hunting, camping, mountain biking, rock climbing, and virtually every kind of recreational pursuit. Silver Creek Ski Area is less than a 1-hour drive from here in winter, and the national forests offer tremendous snowmobiling, cross-country skiing, and snowshoeing opportunities. The Colorado River flows through nearby Lake Granby, providing more great options such as sailing, swimming, or water skiing. There are numerous old mining ghost towns in the area. Some, like Lulu City to the north, are classic examples of a boom-and-bust era in which the life span of a town was measured in years you could count on one hand. There is rich history and even richer recreational opportunity here.

NW 4

Indian Springs

General description: Fully developed historical resort with mud baths and pool.
Location: Thirty minutes west of Denver on Interstate 70.
Development: Pool, lodging, restaurant, and lounge.
Best time to visit: Returning to Denver from a winter skiing trip may be the best.
Restrictions: None.
Access: Easy and convenient year-round access by public roads.
Water temperature: Moderate and variable from 90 to 115 degrees F.
Services: Overnight lodging and food at the resort. Full services in Idaho Springs.
Camping: Yes; hookups available.
Maps: Idaho Springs Quadrangle; Arapaho National Forest; Pike National Forest.
GPS coordinates: N 40 04 29 W 106 06 41.
Finding the springs: From Denver, drive west on I-70 and take exit 241 for Idaho Springs, which will put you onto Colorado Boulevard, the main east-west road through town. Driving west a few blocks you will turn onto Miner Street, heading south to Soda Creek Road, which goes under the interstate. Indian Springs is just ahead on your left.

Overview: The thought that first comes to mind when I think of Indian Springs is *convenience*. It is but a half-hour drive from Colorado's largest city, and directly on the route that thousands of alpine skiers drive every day in the mass winter migration to and from ski areas west of Denver. It is also unique in that it offers mud baths of the type more common in Europe. With a long and varied history dating back to the middle of the nineteenth century, this is an interesting and comfortable destination.

Soda Creek, which runs near the resort, once marked the neutral ground between the Ute and Arapaho Indians, who did not always get along famously. The hot springs were an accepted "free zone" where both tribes could take advantage of the warm, healing influences of the mineral waters bubbling out of the ground, without fear of confrontation.

For centuries, the springs seemed content to produce mineral-laden waters without intervention or argument from humans, but that changed in about 1859 when George Jackson was the first to report gold in a stream nearby. Jackson's Diggins became the name of the town that sprouted with the news of

Indian Springs, Eldorado Springs

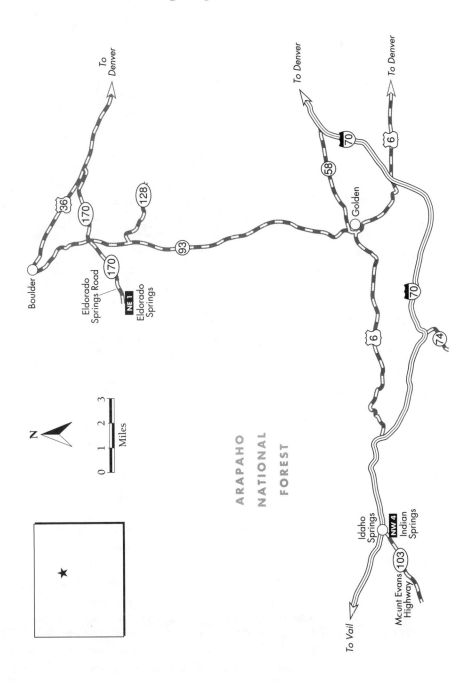

the gold nugget he found on Chicago Creek. The town later was named Idaho, which finally evolved into Idaho Springs. This area was poked and prodded in every crevice by miners of that era, and the hot springs certainly were a welcome luxury to a rough-hewn lifestyle. As early as 1863, a formal structure was built by Dr. E. M. Cummings, who bought the property for its hot-water mine— which had frustrated miners seeking gold in their tunnels, not hot water. Cummings charged the public for access to his wood-framed bathhouse, but in two years he sold it to Harrison Montague, who built a stone structure to re-place the wooden one and called it the Ocean Bath House. In 1869, Montague built what remains today as a central part of the hotel. Throughout the follow-ing years, Indian Springs saw other owners and developers who added or sub-tracted pieces of history. It stands today as an assemblage of both old and new.

In the main building, the hot springs pool is a unique enclosed green-house garden environment with banana and other palm trees and a rock gar-den. Fed by a continual influx of spring water at about 115 degrees F, the over-all temperature of the main pool is about 90 degrees. There is a separate, smaller inset pool that is much warmer for soaking as you enjoy the tropical ambiance of the greenhouse. There are poolside picnic tables with a cabana flavor, and an area used for banquets and privately arranged parties such as wedding recep-tions. The main pool area is large, clean, and family oriented.

Besides the main pool, you may enjoy private baths in tubs about eight feet long, four feet wide, and three feet deep. The baths are equipped with showers, a bench, and 106-degree water.

Down below are the geothermal caves. Dating back to the early miners who burrowed for gold, they are tunnels cut into solid bedrock, with floor-level soaking pools of assorted sizes. In the European tradition they are restricted to nude bathing only, but are segregated for men and women. If you talk to Everett, a man on the maintenance staff at Indian Springs, you may coax a story from him about how the tunnels were once not segregated and the looping tunnel was once simply separated on the honor system. There is a steel gate there now. The vapor caves are humid, warm, and quiet. Except for the hot-water pools, you might imagine how a gopher or mole might feel—securely nestled in the dim warmth of the earth—and how foreign and distant the world above ground suddenly becomes as you sink into the moist heat of the cave baths.

Even more unique is the "Club Mud," as it is called locally. You can cover yourself with smooth mud and feel the absorptive qualities. An old remedy for bee stings is to apply a mudpack, which draws the poison from your skin. The mudrooms feature full-body-size mudpacks, and a trip into artistic expression as well, since tradition holds that you may draw designs and pictures on the walls. Is this finger-painting with no rules? With all the options available to you at Indian Springs you will be steeped, soaked, mudded, and bathed so that

Indian Springs is an easy drive from Denver.

every pore in your skin has been opened. Naturally, there are numerous massage options as well, on the off chance you still have a hint of stress remaining.

The resort has a dining room, a lounge that sometimes features live music, and a variety of old and newer rooms, including some that are handicapped accessible. It is an unassuming, comfortable facility, and a simply wonderful place to soothe skiing bruises on the way back home from the hills, or to relax for an evening retreat only a short drive from downtown Denver.

Area highlights: As close as Indian Springs is to Denver, it also functions as a gateway to the mountain recreational areas. Denver is the state's center for government, commerce, and culture. To the west of Idaho Springs is the multitude of ski areas and high peaks that have made Colorado famous, with mountains for every level of hiker, climber, angler, and hunter.

The Arapaho National Forest provides a wealth of opportunity for snowmobilers, four-wheel-drive and ATV explorers, river-runners, and wildlife viewers. There is a rich history of early mining and American Indian influences nearby as well. Just outside Idaho Springs you can take the Oh My God Road for some spectacular vistas. You can pan for gold in the streams or tour the Argo Gold Mill, listed on the register of National Historic Places. There are a number of "Fourteeners" in this area of Colorado, if 14,000-feet-high mountains are your challenge.

NW 5

South Canyon Hot Springs

General description: Undeveloped hillside hot-pots with a view.
Location: Just west of Glenwood Springs, off Interstate 70 in west-central Colorado.
Development: Undeveloped except for a few rocks conveniently placed.
Best time to visit: This is generally a summertime location because of its exposure to the elements and roadside passers-by when the creek-bottom trees lose their privacy-lending leaves to the changing season.
Restrictions: None.
Access: Nearby access on public roads, but a short trail walk is required.
Water temperature: Moderate and variable, estimated at 112 degrees F at source.
Services: Nearest full services are in Glenwood Springs five miles to the east.
Camping: No hookups or camping facilities.
Maps: Storm King Mountain Quadrangle; White River National Forest.
GPS coordinates: N 39 33 11 W 107 24 40.
Finding the springs: From I-70 five miles west of Glenwood Springs, take exit 111 to County Road 134 (South Canyon Creek Road) to the south. Just after you exit the interstate you will cross the Colorado River, and from that point continue 0.5 mile and watch for a small turnout on your right, at the side of the paved road. There is no sign or other indication of the springs other than footpaths leading down to the creek, which then lead back up the hill about 300 yards. The hot springs pools are on the hillside.

Overview: Some of the most unique and enjoyable hot springs are not known to many, which is of course part of their allure. South Canyon Hot Springs is just such a place; it is known almost exclusively by the locals and intentionally not advertised. Many such places in the American West may never be described in a book because their very existence is a closely guarded secret. The lack of development may exclude some visitors who prefer hot showers and a snack bar, but for those who enjoy a natural setting to complement their naturally heated water, this may be just the place. Accessible, but not for those unwilling to search just a bit or get a little mud between their toes, it is a picturesque location with a great view of the open countryside.

Directly to the north on the near horizon is Storm King Mountain (elevation 13,749 feet) which bears a sad legacy of heroic firefighters and their deaths from wildfire. This is sobering food for thought while you soak. You will see no

South Canyon Hot Springs, Glenwood Hot Springs, Yampah Spa and Vapor Caves

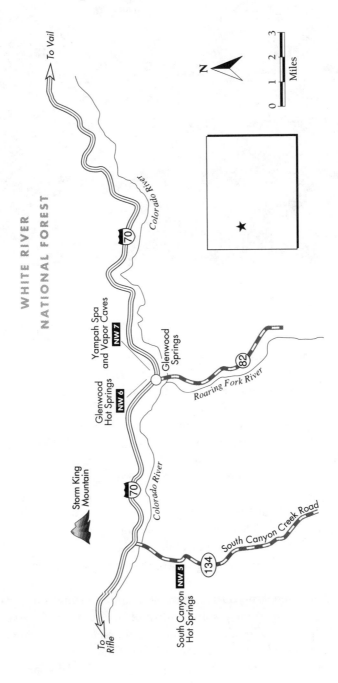

South Canyon Hot Springs offers a secluded view.

houses, motels, or filling stations from your hillside perch, and it will seem crowded if you must share the pool with more than two or three others. There are actually three separate springs, but just two pools are dug out enough for soaking. The larger pool is about 15 feet in diameter and four feet deep at its deepest point. The perimeter is grasses and flat rocks, which make for a delightful seating area.

Because of its relative seclusion, this is an obvious place for clothing-optional rules. In practice, many who enjoy an undeveloped, natural setting such as South Canyon Hot Springs also find it a fitting opportunity to shed their clothes. Unless you are quite new to the clan of regular hot-potters, it seems entirely appropriate here. On a late midsummer evening when the sky is clear, there may be nothing better than slipping into one of the hillside pools to watch the sky turn pink before the stars come out, with no city lights to detract from their brilliance. Secluded, peaceful, and filled with the smells of fresh grass and trees, this may be exactly what hot springs pools were intended to be.

Area highlights: Look no further than the beautiful Glenwood Canyon a few miles to the east for some inspiring work of nature. Carved by centuries of water and silt in the Colorado River, you will find that the sheer canyon walls of stratified rock provide a wondrous automobile tour.

Glenwood Hot Springs Pool is a sterling example of a resort area that has developed around a hot springs, and it boasts first-class facilities—public swimming, restaurants, and athletic clubs. Historically, the area around South Canyon is rich with gold and silver mining, as well as a marble quarry. The White River National Forest offers endless outdoor recreational opportunity, with hunting, fishing, hiking, and boating being some of the best. Whitewater rafting or kayaking on the Colorado River is for the adventurous, but there are several golf courses nearby if you prefer just to relax. There are both small and large ski areas within an hour-long winter drive, and hundreds of miles of snowmobile trails to explore. No matter what the season, there is plenty to see and do.

NW 6

Glenwood Hot Springs

(See map on page 33)

General description: Fully developed, premier hot springs and spa of Colorado.
Location: West of Denver and northeast of Grand Junction on Interstate 70.
Development: Large pools, athletic club, restaurants, and hotels.
Best time to visit: Any time of year is good.
Restrictions: None.
Access: Easy and convenient year-round access by public roads.
Water temperature: Moderate and variable, from 90 to 104 degrees F.
Services: Glenwood Springs has a full range of services.
Camping: None.
Maps: Glenwood Springs Quadrangle; White River National Forest.
GPS coordinates: N 39 33 02 W 107 19 04.
Finding the springs: Glenwood Hot Springs is visible from I-70. Take exit 116 and go north one block, then east—it is impossible to miss. From Grand Junction it is 90 miles to the east on I-70, and from Denver, 160 miles to the west.

Overview: If you had a speedboat, you could almost water ski in the larger of the two pools at Glenwood Hot Springs, and hardly anyone might notice. At 405 feet long and 100 feet wide, it is not only the largest natural hot springs-fed pool in Colorado, it is one of the largest anywhere on the planet. Size is not the measure of grandeur, but certainly this qualifies as Colorado's premier hot springs resort for a host of good reasons. In a world of marketing hype and overblown claims to greatness, Glenwood Hot Springs is genuinely world class. It is a destination that can claim a long and impressive list of visitors including Ute Indian chiefs, early miners, gunfighters, and American presidents. Some of the world's most wealthy, famous, and infamous people have spent time appreciating Glenwood.

Producing more than 3.5 million gallons of hot water (122 degree F) every day, Yampah Hot Springs has a fascinating history. So named for the Ute Indian term that translates "Big Medicine," the springs produces enough water to create a small river from the earth.

The unusually hot water is used to refresh the pools every few hours, but it is tempered by blending it with cool water that drops the temperature to about 90 degrees—tolerable to tender human skin. The larger pool contains more than one million gallons of water that is completely replaced every six hours. The smaller pool, measuring 100 feet in length and no small puddle in its own right, is kept at approximately 104 degrees and is considered the therapy pool. The smaller pool experiences a complete replacement of its 91,000 gallons every two hours. Even with the constant influx of replacement water, the big pool has been filtered with a state-of-the-art ozone disinfection system since 1991 as an extra measure to keep it sparkling clean. There's still enough hot water flowing to heat the lodge and spa with the warmth, making it the largest building in Colorado to be heated with geothermal energy.

The pool complex has just about everything anyone could want in a resort swimming facility. There are lap lanes, a diving area at the 12-foot depth, a water slide, and a kiddie pool. The shallow end, with a depth of about three feet, is large enough that most of the town of Glenwood Springs could baby-sit its kids there all at once. The smaller "therapy pool" is lined with underwater benches and stairs, making it perfect for soaking weary, overworked muscles, or for simply relaxing from a day's stress. Though the pools are both comfortable all year long, the hot pool is especially luxurious during the winter months when the air is cool and snow blankets the surrounding mountains. Winter at Glenwood Springs is mild enough for many outdoor hot springs activities, especially considering the elevation is in excess of 5,700 feet above sea level, but summer is a great season to take advantage of the spacious deck terraces and lounging areas for sunning. There are shady "greens" to hide under when the rays become too intense at high noon.

The Hot Springs Athletic Club is part of the resort and features a wide selection of activities including racquetball, weight lifting, and aerobics that may prompt you to seek the relief of that cozy therapy pool after you've flogged your muscles a bit. If you forgot your swimsuit or your towel, you can rent those, too, or maybe take advantage of the assorted massage treatments. You can spoil yourself with a deep-pore facial; Swedish, Thai, and polarity massages;

The pool at Glenwood Hot Springs is big enough to set sail in.

or maybe a foot reflexology session. You can browse in the sport and gift shop, have a snack at the restaurant, or putter about the mini-golf course. The club is so comprehensive, there's even a cash machine. The water-analysis spec sheet available at the front desk or at the lodge details a complex mineral composition to the water, if that sort of thing interests you, but all you really may care about is that this is a wonderfully complete resort for all ages, any time of the year.

If you arrive at Glenwood Springs via I-70 from the east, you will already have enjoyed a fascinating trip through human and geologic history, as well as feasted your eyes on 18 miles of nature's awesome craftwork. The 800-feet-deep canyon walls are a labyrinth of quartzite, limestone, and granite. Carved over the millennia by the Colorado River, Glenwood Canyon is a profile of Colorado geology in its tectonic shifts, faults, the erosive ravages of wind, acid, groundwater, and tides from long receded oceans. In October 1887, at the culmination of two years of labor and after the expenditure of what was then the astounding sum of 2 million dollars, the first Denver and Rio Grande train arrived on new railroad tracks through Glenwood Canyon. The blasting scars are still visible today in the long memory of rock walls. More recently, amid a vocal storm of controversy, the interstate highway was built over a 12-year period at a cost of 490 million dollars. In an effort to appease everyone, the Colorado Senate mandated that the highway be built in such a way as to blend the wonder of human engineering with that of nature. Ultimately, the project has won numerous national and international awards for its design, engineering, and environmental sensitivity. This highway has allowed millions of travelers to witness the even more extraordinary work of Mother Nature in Glenwood Canyon, and to sample a bit of the human history that so colors the area around Glenwood Hot Springs.

The railroad was an integral part of the development of Glenwood Springs, but earlier, during European settlement of the area, a man by the name of Richard Sopris is believed to have been the first white man to visit the hot springs. In 1860 he named the place Grand Springs, which held until 1883 when prospectors from Aspen and Leadville bestowed the name of Defiance on the fort they built to defend themselves against the Ute Indians, who still frequented the area. In typical mining-town fashion, it grew as a town of tents, and shacks, and thrown-together buildings that harbored gamblers, harlots, and miners.

In 1885, Isaac Cooper came west from Iowa and formed a company called the Defiance Town and Cattle Company. The company purchased 400 acres as the site for a township, which Isaac named Glenwood (after his hometown in Iowa), only to have it later renamed Glenwood Springs by his wife, Sarah. Cooper was instrumental in bringing the railroad to Glenwood Springs, but he died prior to realizing his vision of developing a world-class spa there. That honor fell to Walter Devereaux, a well-financed engineer with an East Coast education; Devereaux had learned about the springs from mountain man Kit Carson. He rerouted the Colorado River, developed the vapor caves, and oversaw the building of the stone pool and natatorium, along with the Hotel Colorado. This industrious fellow even started a polo club for the growing community of well-heeled and well-known patrons.

In 1887, famous gunfighter Doc Holliday, suffering from consumption, became a resident of Glenwood Springs, seeking peace and the hope of restorative power in the Yampah Hot Springs. He died of tuberculosis at the age of 35 and is buried in Pioneer Cemetery, which overlooks the central part of town. The Hotel Colorado opened in 1893 and became the social epicenter for notables that included President Theodore Roosevelt, who came to the area to hunt bear and other big game. Disheartened at being unable to find a bear, Teddy was cheered by the hotel maids who put together a little bear from cloth scraps as a consolation gift, and the "Teddy Bear" was suddenly established in history. Over the years, Glenwood Hot Springs has bathed luminaries such as Al Capone, Diamond Jim Brady, President Taft, Grover Cleveland, and "Buffalo Bill" (William Frederick Cody). It is genuinely a "destination."

Area highlights: Before you even leave the hot springs themselves, you will have been afforded an impressive array of entertaining options. The health club and the local history of the Hotel Colorado and the town of Glenwood Springs are intriguing for visitors. Ski Sunlight is a locally accessible destination for down-hill and cross-country skiers, but world-famous Aspen and Beaver Creek ski resorts are but a one-hour drive away. There is the impressive Glenwood Canyon, whitewater rafting on the Colorado River, excellent fishing in the Frying Pan and Roaring Fork rivers or Ruedi Reservoir, and wonderful hiking, biking, and ATV trails and tracks to explore in all directions. Golfing in and around Glenwood Springs takes in The Hill, Rifle Creek, Westbank Ranch, and Battlement Mesa, all impressive courses that feature beautiful mountain scenery. You might be interested in visiting the marble quarry; the very pure marble quarried here was used in the Lincoln Memorial and the Tomb of the Unknown Soldier. There are dude ranches, rodeos, and a summertime strawberry festival. Winter hosts snowmobiling and some of the best ice climbing in the west. Whether you are a hunter, hiker, climber, or simply a drive-by tourist, a wealth of adventure awaits you in the Glenwood Hot Springs area.

NW 7

Yampah Spa and Vapor Caves

(See map on page 33)

General description: Hot spring-fed vapor caves and spa salon.
Location: Northwest Colorado on Interstate 70 at Glenwood Springs.
Development: Underground caves and spa facilities with solarium and bathhouse.
Best time to visit: Any time of year, since the caves are underground.
Restrictions: None.
Access: Easy and convenient year-round access by public roads.
Water temperature: Hot and variable, from 110 to 125 degrees F.
Services: Full services are available in Glenwood Springs.
Camping: None.
Maps: Glenwood Springs Quadrangle; White River National Forest.
GPS coordinates: N 39 33 03 W 107 19 11.
Finding the springs: The Yampah Vapor Caves are visible from I-70. Take exit 116 and travel north a block, then east on Sixth Street past the big Glenwood Hot Springs pool complex. The Vapor Caves are a few blocks ahead. The site is located 90 miles east of Grand Junction on I-70, and 160 miles west of Denver.

Overview: With a heritage that precedes recorded history, the Yampah Vapor Caves are the only known natural steam chambers in America. Long known about and used by the native peoples, they were fought over and used for both healing and sometimes punishment by the Arapaho, Utes, and Cheyenne Indians. In an area blessed with numerous hydrogeologic formations, the planet's inner depths bring their magma close to the surface here. The hot springs water flows through the vapor caves at a searing 125 degrees, creating steam vapor laden with minerals leached from the heart of the mountains. Generally regarded as rejuvenative, the mineral waters have a very faint sulfurous aroma to remind you of their purported healing ability. In these days of lawsuits and finger-pointing, nobody will guarantee the healthful benefits of mineral hot springs. But as the Yampah Caves celebrates its centennial, with little effort you can find a legion of believers and a very long history of supporters. In its present use, the spa provides a lesson in pampering yourself, offering every conceivable health and beauty process.

More than most mineral-springs developments, the waters of the Glenwood Springs region seem to have a history of promising great restorative power. Perhaps that's why they were popular enough with the Indians to fight over, why Doc Holliday, the famous gunfighter and dentist, sought this area as his hoped-for salvation (he died of tuberculosis in Glenwood Springs in 1887), and why the caves enjoy such staunch support. Consider *The Bancroft Manuscript,* which spoke in the late 1800s of the remarkable waters: "One of the most singular things about the use of the waters is the certainty with which it brings back to bald heads a full head of hair. This is done inside of three months by rubbing with the water once daily." Reputed to be a virtual panacea, the mineral water of these springs were said to be a cure for "ailments of the flesh" ranging from

rheumatism and gout to lead poisoning, obesity, and pimples. People gargled with it, drank it, soaked in it, and inhaled its vapors. Evidently some people even rubbed it on their heads. Perhaps Juan Ponce de Leon should have sought his fountain of youth in the Colorado mountains instead of the Florida coast.

Despite the legacy of remedies and miracles, the real value of these caves may be less dramatic but much more viable. Descending the stairway at Yampah Caves, you will discover a sanctuary of quiet warmth and a virtual cornucopia of massage and beauty treatments that leave you feeling as if you have emerged from the womb: clean, fresh, and untarnished.

The original caves (numbering three) have been expanded and civilized from the days when men, carrying a candle, would crawl into a tunnel in the morning, and women, unaccompanied by men, would do the same in the afternoon, wearing a linen sack tied at the neck in deference to the modesty of the times. The adjoining rock chambers have an atmosphere of hushed mystery, reminding you of the first time you went to church when nobody else was there.

But these chambers are steamy and hot, averaging 100 to 112 degrees F. There are one-hundred-year-old marble-slab benches to recline upon as you absorb heat and mineral vapors in the dim light. Cooling rooms and small cool-water tubs are available for temperature control if you get too warm. Extensively renovated in 1990, the fixtures, wiring, and plumbing were upgraded and now include a solarium upstairs to relax in after your "vapor time." There is a feeling that you have been invited into the warm, silent depths of the earth. It is relaxing embrace.

This is a pampering place, make no mistake. Other areas of the building feature herbal whirlpool baths and hot tubs, segregated shower and dressing facilities, and personal care services including Swedish and Esalan massages, herbal facials, full-body mud packs, herbal body wraps, loofa body scrubs, rose petal body masques, salt glow rubs, facial tonifications, hair waxing, manicures, pedicures, foot reflexology, and even a plain old haircut. Wow. You can go in feeling beaten-up and corroded, like an old lead pipe crusted over with barnacles, and come out with every pore cleansed, rubbed, scrubbed, and herbalized, with nary a shred of stress remaining in your shiny body. Speaking from experience, even an hour in the vapor caves is enough to replace a stressed, tense attitude with a mellow outlook on life.

The history of the Yampah Caves is inseparable from that of nearby Glenwood Hot Springs, and makes for interesting conjecture while you breathe the same vapors that ancient civilizations and old lead-poisoned miners once did. If you exit the Yampah Caves anything but relaxed and scrubbed, you have only yourself to blame.

Area highlights: When you are not becoming a limp noodle at the Yampah Vapor Caves, you can stroll over to the Glenwood Hot Springs resort for another impressive array of entertaining options, including restaurants, a health club, and Colorado's premier hot springs pools. The local history of the Hotel Colorado and the town of Glenwood Springs are really interesting; including a lengthy list of famous folks who have spent time here. In winter, there are many places to enjoy the superb scenery from aboard a snowmobile, on cross-country skis, or while schussing down the slopes of Aspen, Beaver Creek, or Ski Sunlight ski areas. Ice-climbers consider this area a destination as well. The legendary Colorado River roars through the beautiful Glenwood Canyon and offers whitewater rafting, canoeing, and kayaking from here to Mexico. You can wet a fly on the Roaring Fork and Frying Pan rivers or sail on Ruedi Reservoir. The White River National Forest is full of outdoor recreational opportunities like camping, hunting, angling, hiking, horseback trail riding, and exploring on foot or with your ATV, mountain bike, or your four-wheel-drive vehicle. There are golf courses, summer festivals (like the Strawberry Festival—a 100-year-old tradition), and rodeos. You need not be bored.

NW 8

Conundrum Hot Springs

General description: A secluded collection of pools in a beautiful wilderness location.
Location: Northwestern Colorado, just outside Aspen in the Maroon Bells–Snowmass Wilderness.
Development: Essentially undeveloped, wilderness location.
Best times to visit: Summer and early fall.
Restrictions: Wilderness access only—no motorized or mechanical vehicles.
Access: Aggressive 9-mile hike each way, but trail is generally well marked.
Water temperature: Moderate and variable from about 100 to 105 degrees F.
Services: Aspen offers the nearest full services.
Camping: Camping is the only overnight option. No vehicles allowed.
Maps: Maroon Bells Quadrangle; Hayden Peak Quadrangle; White River National Forest; San Isabel National Forest; Gunnison National Forest.
GPS coordinates: N 39 00 43 W 106 53 27.

Finding the springs: From Aspen, drive north on State Highway 82 less than .5 mile, watching for Forest Service Road 102 (Maroon Creek Road) on your left (if you cross the bridge on SH 82 over Maroon Creek, you have gone too far!). Promptly turn left again onto Castle Creek Road and drive south about 5 miles on winding paved road. On your right, look for Conundrum Road, which drops downhill and soon changes to gravel. Keep to the left as you cross the creek, and follow the signs to the trailhead about 1 mile farther. Private property along the route is heavily posted and area landowners have been quick to have illegally parked vehicles towed, so park *only* at the trailhead. The last mile is best suited to four-wheel-drive vehicles during the muddy spring and winter.

Overview: You have spent the autumn afternoon outdoors, and you come into the house to smell roast turkey and homemade bread baking in the oven. It is still a couple of hours till supper, and after a day of brisk air, the aroma is making your mouth water. As the time for the dinner bell grows near, the sweet anticipation piqued by the wonderful scents can only be surpassed by a slab of juicy roast bird and a thick slice of warm bread slathered in butter.

Conundrum Hot Springs offers the same experience in many ways. The anticipation and temptation is part of the enjoyment in the end. In the case of Conundrum, you must earn your pleasure because the hike is not for the faint of heart—or legs and lungs. According to the map, it is roughly 9 miles from the trailhead to the lowest of the springs. With a beginning elevation of nearly 9,000 feet, the air begins to thin and your body seems a little less perky from a diminished oxygen supply. Almost immediately after leaving the parking lot, you will cross into the Maroon Bells–Snowmass Wilderness, where no bicycles or motor devices or mechanical transport are allowed. In other words, that means you walk or take a horse to your destination.

At the outset the mountains are high and beautiful, framing the Conundrum Creek drainage with peaks littered by waterfalls, rocky edifices, and aspen groves. The peaks beckon with their beauty. The first part of the trail is relatively easy and moderate in elevation changes. Though the hot springs are nearly 3,000 feet higher than where you start, most of the ascent is fairly gradual, with the majority of the elevation gain experienced toward the end of the hike. You will follow the creek all the way to Conundrum Hot Springs.

Depending on whom you talk to, this is a difficult hike or it is simply a good day's outing in God's country. Take time for a reality check before you venture out with expectations of going there and back in one day. If you have not seen your toes in a few years and most of your exercise comes with scrambling for the TV remote control, this is not going to be easy for you. If you exercise regularly and ten-minute-miles in the 10K run are standard fare for you, you will probably have no trouble. The good news is, if you make the

Conundrum Hot Springs

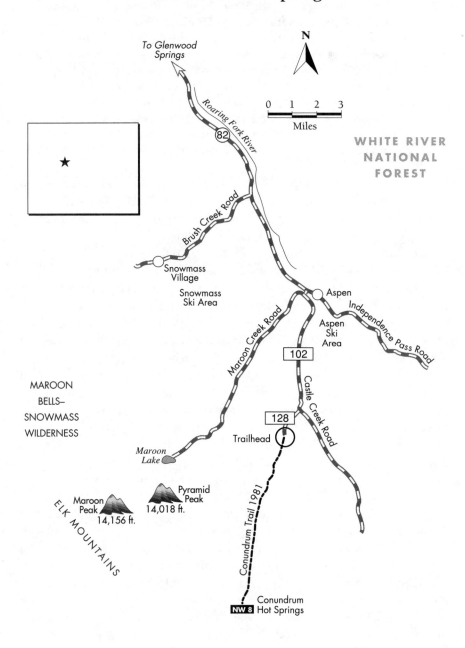

Conundrum Hot Springs is paradise on a mountain top.

effort and come up short of your destination, you still will have enjoyed gorgeous scenery every step of the way. Remember, this is 9 miles each way!

The best advice I can give for hiking into Conundrum is to pick your weather carefully and make sure your hiking boots are well broken in. At these elevations, the weather can change from a bluebird day to a blizzard in a matter of hours. Plan ahead and allow yourself plenty of time, not only to get there, but to enjoy the springs and have adequate time for the return trip or setting up camp. I will not try to turn this section of the book into a hiker's guide with pack lists and hiking advice, but the trip can be a good challenge. Just for the sake of reference, my most recent trip into Conundrum in late June of 1998 was with an inexperienced backpacking partner. We left the trailhead after noon and were back to my truck before dark, after soaking and relaxing for an hour in the pools. That's an 18-mile day, but quite achievable for anyone with good lungs and enough determination. If you can find a suitable camping spot, it is much better to relax and stay overnight, enjoying the springs longer.

Perhaps the conundrum in Conundrum Hot Springs is the popularity of this location. Despite being a modestly challenging destination, it is surprising how many people you can find up there in late summer. You probably will not have the place completely to yourself, although on my last trip there were only two other soakers at the springs, and the other pools were quite empty. It is clear that on a holiday weekend or when the weather is predictably good, the place can see more visitors than it can properly handle.

Camping with campfires is not allowed within about a mile or so of the springs. High alpine environments are fragile, which makes them susceptible to abuse. This is a quandary that public land administrators wrestle with constantly. Insensitive abuse of the land will certainly result in restrictions such as a permit system or an area closure. Remember to obey all the signs for camping in designated locations, deal with your refuse properly, and practice low-impact rules of conduct. Check with the regional Forest Service office for guidelines on wilderness use, for certainly Conundrum suffers the indignity of slob hikers and campers. As beautiful as the Maroon Bells and Conundrum Hot Springs can be, overuse and misuse can spoil the site for everyone.

All of that said, Conundrum is still one of Colorado's most exquisite settings, and if you pick your time carefully, your visit there can be an outstanding, secluded experience. The pools vary in size and temperature, but the larger pools average about 102 degrees F, depending on the season. Some small pools are fed by a length of plastic pipe from higher sources, and they are cooler. The pools are craters of rock hewn into their present shape over years of visitation, and they make for great soaking. The larger pools are more than 3 feet deep and have room for several people, if need be. No matter which pool you fancy or which direction you face, you will have superb views of the surrounding rocky spires and alpine terrain. Steep avalanche chutes and pockets of snow that almost never leave, waterfalls, and the bright greens and flowers of short-life-span plants are all around you.

If you feel that you are on top of the world, its because you nearly are, at nearly 12,000 feet in elevation. Look down the long valley you have just ascended and marvel at the clear view and the expanse of beauty while you soak in your little hot pot high in the wilderness. It's the same view that early miners and native Indians savored for generations. If you stay for the night and are blessed with clear skies, you may be dazzled by the sight of more stars than you ever thought existed, seemingly so close you can reach out and take one to guide your way back to the tent. You might ask yourself if life could get any better. Savor the pure pleasure of clear, high mountain air and the tingle in your toes that says you have earned this view and the soothing warmth of water nearly perfect in temperature.

Conundrum Hot Springs lives up to its name. On a bad day, you are simply embarrassed to be a human, in view of the litter and apparent disregard for nature's fragile wonders. On a good day, it is the very definition of a great hot springs.

Area highlights: Aspen, Colorado has a reputation for being home to some wealthy and famous people, but the benefit to you is a nice choice of restaurants and services in town.

Aspen, Snowmass, and Buttermilk Ski areas are right there for your winter enjoyment, and the high elevation promises plenty of snow for cross-country skiing, snowmobiling, and winter hikes. The nearby Maroon Bells–Snowmass Wilderness is known as one of Colorado's most scenic, but not far away are the Mount Massive, Holy Cross, and Collegiate Peaks wilderness areas. The San Isabel, White River, and Gunnison national forests offer endless outdoor recreation, from fishing, hiking, and hunting to climbing any of several "Fourteeners" (14,000-feet-high peaks) nearby. If you just want to see some spectacular mountain scenery from the comfort of your car, take a summer drive over Independence Pass (elevation 12,095 feet). Ruedi Reservoir, Turquoise Lake, and Twin Lakes Reservoir offer water sports on a larger scale, or you can enjoy whitewater adventure in countless rivers and creeks from the Arkansas to the Gunnison rivers. Aspen has a history as an old mining town, producing gold and silver ore worth more than $10 million by 1889. The largest silver nugget in Colorado came from the Smuggler mine; it weighed over a ton! Nearby Independence and Ashcroft were part of the mining history, but are little more than ghost towns now. Surrounded by mountain beauty in all directions, this is a recreational paradise for everyone.

NORTHEAST COLORADO
HOT SPRINGS

NE 1

Eldorado Springs

(See map on page 29)

General description: Historically significant, fully developed swimming pool and bottled water business.

Location: Just south of Boulder and west of Denver in north-central Colorado.

Development: Swimming pool, changing rooms, and snack bar. Bottled water plant.

Best time to visit: A warm-water springs—best in summer.

Restrictions: None.

Access: Easy and convenient year-round access by public roads.

Water temperature: Moderate to cool, from 72 to 82 degrees F.

Services: Snacks and locally bottled water. Full services nearby in Boulder.

Camping: None.

Maps: Eldorado Quadrangle; Arapaho National Forest; Roosevelt National Forest.

GPS coordinates: N 39 55 56 W 105 16 47.

Finding the springs: Take State Highway 93 south out of Boulder to its junction with State Highway 170 (also known as Eldorado Springs Drive). Turn onto SH 170 and head west 3.5 miles to Eldorado Springs, heading straight into the mouth of Eldorado Springs Canyon. There are signs to direct you as you near Eldorado Springs.

An alternative route, coming from Denver, is to take West Sixth Avenue from the heart of the city driving west to Golden. Just past Golden (home of Coors Beer)—you will be heading generally northwest—you will intersect State Highway 58 briefly before you are on SH 93 heading north toward Boulder. Just before you would get to Boulder, take the turnoff onto SH 170 (Eldorado Springs Road) heading west, as described above.

Overview: In the history of hot springs, artesian wells, and cool-water springs throughout Colorado, few waters have nearly the colorful background that Eldorado Springs can claim.

Eldorado Springs—great water to swim in or drink.

As a work of nature, Eldorado Springs has bubbled happily for countless ages, long before recorded history. The Colorado Ute Indians found this setting to their liking, and probably for the same reasons that we do today. The ancestors of the Utes, in whatever hominid form they took, doubtless watered at the very same place. That is likely because this percolating springs has seeping and artesian elements to it, and barring an earthquake of cataclysmic proportions, it has probably been around since our ancestors were one-celled creatures in the primordial ooze. More recent history would include events such as the arrival of wagon trains headed for the promised lands. They would stop to chase away the "savages" and claim ownership of the springs for themselves. Wagon boss Charlie Barber did just that, and he managed to relieve much of the surrounding canyon of its trees, too. Boom and bust cycles seem to have been the story of Eldorado Springs, but always the sweet, pure water has flowed, despite the silliness of human activity above ground.

Situated in the mouth of Eldorado Canyon beside South Boulder Creek and next to Eldorado State Park, the area immediately west of Eldorado Springs is also a destination for rock climbers who challenge the canyon's rock walls in technical gear and free ascents. On a given day, but especially in the summertime, you might see a dozen or more climbers clinging to the steep canyon cliffs like so many flies on the kitchen wall. This is a climbing zone for gaining "extreme" experience or for learning some of the fundamentals, whether it is on the Bastille or the Naked Edge. As you drive out of the Eastern Front prairie into the mountains, you will witness an abrupt change in topography, the mountains leaping suddenly and steeply out of the earth. Part of the attraction to the surroundings here is the beautiful rocky outcrops and cliffs; besides being a magnet to the climbing community, this is a wonderfully accessible hiking and sightseeing area. It is a visual picnic.

If during a summer day you are watching all the rock climbers tempt fate and the air temperature reaches the mid-70s or above, you'll likely see a happy swarm of people in and around the pool, enjoying the fact that this is not a hot springs but is instead a *warm* springs. An owner and do-it-all manager of water-bottling operations, Kevin Sipple, says the water temperature in the pool runs between 72 and 82 degrees F, depending on the seasonal influences. By hot-springs standards that's downright chilly, but for the legions of kids and the adults who brought them, it is sweet summertime relief. Eldorado Springs is unassuming, casual, and close enough to the metropolitan areas of Denver and Boulder that it is a reachable destination far more special than the municipal pool back in town. Tucked into the shadow of the towering mountains to the west and guarded from overheating by their protection, the springs provides a wonderful escape from the congestion and swelter of the city. There are huge old shade trees all about, and knowing something about the colorful history adds to the experience. The mildly alternative-lifestyle community in which Eldorado Springs nestles seems to guard the historic landmark with a proprietary appreciation.

At one time this spot was known as the Coney Island of Colorado. After the wagon trains left, a group of "spiritual visionaries" and "introspective travelers" set up camp at Eldorado, followed around 1904 by Fowler's Moffat Lakes Resort. The steep canyon and its pool, which was the only official swimming pool in all of Colorado until after 1920, was becoming a major attraction. In the early 1900s the Denver and Interurban Electric Line was bringing hundreds of people to visit on the weekends.

The year 1907 saw an interesting figure arrive on the scene—Ivy Baldwin, also known as the Human Fly. His daring tightrope traverse of the 635-feet-wide span across the lower end of the canyon was done almost 90 times, to the sheer amazement of all who could appreciate the drop of 582 feet to the canyon floor. Strategically anchored in the rocks, his high-wire made it possible for people to witness the spectacle of this daredevil showman from the Springs. Ivy was known to have done aerial reconnaissance surveys from hot air balloons in the Spanish Civil War. He was evidently either quite nuts or possessed of enormous courage and athletic skill; it was probably the latter, in view of the fact that he died quietly in his bed at the age of 82.

In 1908 an impressive hotel was built, attracting such public figures as movie star Mary Pickford and world heavyweight boxing champion Jack Dempsey (who held the world title from 1919–1926). Like many old wooden buildings in history, the hotel succumbed to a devastating fire, but another structure was built on its ashes. Dwight and Mamie Eisenhower spent part of their honeymoon at Eldorado Springs, and Glenn Miller got everybody in the mood when he and his orchestra were top billing at about the time of World War II. From a cool watering spring for the Ute Indians to a high-profile, high-society gathering place, over the years Eldorado Springs has seen it all.

In spite of its glamorous and varied history and a nice large pool with lifeguards on duty, it is the spring water that makes Eldorado a working concern in this modern time.

Kevin Sipple estimates nearly a thousand 5-gallon containers leave Eldorado Springs daily for the Denver metropolitan area. The water is pure enough to need no filtration, and its natural carbonation keeps intruding bacteria at bay. The pool and snack bar ride the shirttails of the bottled-water business, and everyone seems happy with the results. Having hotter water might be a pleasant option for some, but in 1933 the drilling effort for hot water came up with cold. As a result, this is a more popular place in summer than the dead of winter. Showing signs of wear, the pool area is still well kept and clean. There are pleasant sundecks and lots of places to explore just a short walk away. Before you leave, be sure to fill your water jugs at the tub out in front of the bottling facility, which charges 25 cents per fill—payment is on the "honor system." That should tell you just how comfortable and easy it is to relax at Eldorado Springs.

Area highlights: This is a busy part of Colorado, and offers more things to do than most of us have time to do them. If outdoor recreation is your interest, the mountains to the west of Denver are at your doorstep from Eldorado Springs. The Arapaho National Forest is bursting with opportunities to enjoy hiking, fishing, rock climbing, hunting, mountain biking, and a host of other outdoor sports. The Flat Iron Range, just outside Boulder, is a uniquely beautiful place to explore. Even if you never get out of your vehicle, you can do some rugged exploration in your four-wheel-drive vehicle or take a cruise up "Oh My God Road" out of Idaho Springs. Mount Evans to the southwest is just one of the nearby peaks reaching 14,000 feet in elevation, and it can be accessed via the Mount Evans Highway for some spectacular views and a better appreciation of the oxygen levels at lower elevations.

If you enjoy poking around old ghost towns, there is an abundance of them nearby. Places like Black Hawk, Central City, Nevadaville, and Idaho Springs are here in the present but still firmly connected to the past, like a walk onto a western movie set with a very real history. Central City is only 34 miles west of Denver, and boasts a remarkable diary of fortune and glamour, being once heralded as the "richest square mile on earth." An extremely prosperous mining area that produced over $70 million in precious metals (mostly gold and silver), it was home to many of Colorado's influential and affluent, becoming a society center back when a train ticket from Denver cost $2.65. President Ulysses S. Grant was astounded on his visit when residents of Central City proudly laid a walkway of silver bars for him to walk on, from the street to the Teller Hotel.

If you seek the culture of the larger urban areas, Denver and the cluster of development that has grown up around Colorado's Queen City have much to offer. There are museums, restaurants, sporting events, and shopping that befits a city the size of the state's capitol. In the near surrounds of Eldorado Springs you might enjoy the variety of breweries, from giant Anheuser-Busch and Coors to a large assortment of micro breweries like Walnut Creek. To the north, a visit to Rocky Mountain National Park will add to your appreciation of the majesty of this awesome country and its wildlife. In winter, there are numerous ski areas that have made skiing and snowboarding a multi-billion dollar industry in Colorado, including Arapaho Basin, Aspen, Vail, and Copper Mountain among the many celebrated centers for winter enthusiasts. In the mountains blessed with so much snow, cross-country skiing and snowmobiling are also quite popular. A visit to Eldorado Springs will be a visit with history, and certainly you will run out of time long before you run out of interesting things to do in the area.

Southeast Colorado Hot Springs

SE 1

The Well at Brush Creek

General description: Semiprivate clothing-optional pool.
Location: About 30 miles west of Pueblo in central-southeast Colorado.
Development: Concrete pool, sun decks, changing area with lounge.
Best time to visit: Winter takes advantage of very moderate cold season.
Restrictions: Clothing-optional, limited membership and entry.
Access: Easy and convenient year-round access by public roads.
Water temperature: Moderate and variable, from 95 to 108 degrees F.
Services: None. Very limited overnight camping.
Camping: Very limited space. No recreation vehicle hookups.
Map: Florence Quadrangle.
GPS coordinates: N 38 24 53 W 105 2 43.
Finding the springs: Drive south of Colorado Springs on Interstate 25 to State Highway 115; take SH 115 southwest to its junction with U.S. Highway 50. Head west on US 50 for 1 mile until you see The Well. There is a large set of white iron stanchions over the access road into The Well off the south side of the highway. If you are traveling west out of Pueblo, simply take US 50 until you meet that same junction in about 27 miles, depending on where you exited Pueblo.

Overview: This is not the Hilton, but you will not find a Hilton that lets you take a bubble bath with all your friends in a 70-foot pool with a gunslinger for the lifeguard. In a geographic zone known as Colorado's "banana belt" because it averages 350 days of sunshine annually and the winters are mild, is an eclectic place in the high desert called The Well. In an area sprinkled with oil wells, The Well is an artesian hot-water well that was abandoned by the Continental Oil Company (Conoco) in 1924 when they found water at a depth of 2,000 feet—instead of the preferred black gold. Evidently the oil company found that to be an unsatisfactory discovery, and in its contempt for non-hydrocarbon fluids, the company simply went off in search of wells that flowed coal juice. The slightly carbonated water flows, at a rate of over 300 gallons per minute, from

The Well at Brush Creek, Desert Reef Beach Club

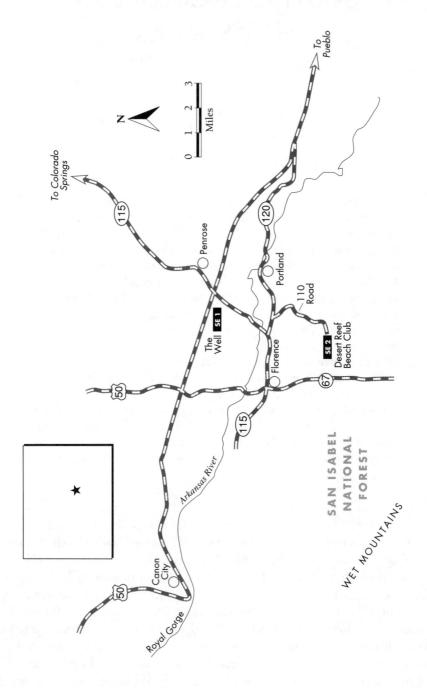

under what was once an old mining claim. The six-foot-diameter round soaking tub is kept at a temperature of about 108 degrees F, but most of the 70-feet-long pool is about 95 degrees.

This is a large pool, with depths ranging from 2 feet to about 5 feet. There is a volleyball net set up on one end and much of the activity seems to focus there. The water itself is relatively low in odorous sulfur compounds, making for pleasant soaking. There's a communal lounging area with a wood stove at its center, and enough glass to keep the temperature comfortable when it is windy or cool outside, but the furnishings are representative of most of The Well's décor, which is to say a bit rough around the edges. Perhaps it might be best to describe this as a work in progress, awaiting copious amounts of money and time to smooth its unpolished ambiance. You might well see a tumbleweed roll by in the breeze, despite roughly hewn and constructed walls of snow fence and old lumber, but the informal, unfinished state doesn't seem to bother the patrons. If it is polish and finery you seek, this is not your spot.

You also need to know that this is very much a clothing-optional facility. Optional means just that, but the theme of being tuned to a different beat than the rest of the world plays here too, because acceptance is gained more readily without clothes than with. That is probably not what you would expect if you walked into Kmart wearing nothing more than your birthday suit. You may find that in an environment where the sexual overtones are diminished and improper behavior simply is not tolerated, that your comfort level while wearing no more than anyone else is surprisingly high.

Manager Grover Simpson is a congenial man who seems slightly out of step with the rest of the world's pace, in a charming, colorful way. Would it seem contrary that a large interest of his is being a member of the Rocky Mountain Gunslingers? Ask him to show you his photo album with a varied collection of street gunfights and assorted hunting adventures mixed with a sprinkling of back-to-nature swimming trips. You might catch this man, who seems to cloak himself in a bit of 1960s spirit, reloading ammunition or joining the swimmers on any given day, but you can be sure he is quite capable of enforcing the "no rowdies" rules. Grover will show you the dozen simple rules printed on the wall at the front office, but in essence they distill down to a very basic mandate to behave yourself and act like an adult, or he will toss you out without so much as a blink. Would you argue with a guy who is a part-time gunslinger? Not many do,

and the demeanor is decidedly relaxed. No glass near the pool and no lewd behavior (Grover decides what is lewd, by the way) or you're toast.

The Well promotes itself as a family operation but it seems to draw mostly adults, and surprisingly, most members are not locals. Daily rates are $5 per person for members and guests of members, with drop-ins (nonmembers) being charged twice that amount.

There are about 250 members of The Well club, and being a resident living more than 100 miles distant reduces your annual dues by $50 for a single membership.

Remember when your mother used to tell you to take a bath at night when you had been out playing all day, but it was still light out? Remember how you hated to take that bath, even when she said you could take Mr. Bubble, your rubber ball, and the yellow rubber ducks in with you? Well, now that you're a little older, you might discover a little treasure in life not too different from the joy of realizing that as an adult you can go to the Dairy Queen as often as you like without asking anyone first. Bubble night at The Well. Every Monday night, members and guests bring bottles of bubble bath and combine to make a glorious, seventy-feet-long bathtub of hot water and foaming waves of bubbles. There is a volleyball net for playing bubbleball, and lots of laughing and frolicking about. And Grover says it's all "okay by me." Talk about good clean fun—who needs Monday Night Football? Will it help you feel more comfortable to know that this happens every Monday night as a prelude to draining the entire pool for its weekly cleaning? Next time you have trouble getting the kids to take their baths, just think about The Well.

Area highlights: In a place that seems full of contradictions, it seems appropriate that The Well would be so free in spirit but exists surrounded by numerous state and federal prison complexes. In nearby Canon City you can visit a unique prison museum or stop in to see the Holy Cross Abbey. The road west takes you to the breathtaking Royal Gorge and the highest suspension bridge in the world, over the Arkansas River.

There is the Pro Rodeo Hall of Fame in Colorado Springs, and endless outdoor activities including fishing, rafting, hunting, and skiing. There is excellent wildlife watching in the areas west of Canon City, and to the north is the Florissant Fossil Beds National Monument and Pikes Peak. Denver is but an afternoon's drive away, and has the tremendous cultural offering that accompanies Colorado's capital city.

SE 2

Desert Reef Beach Club

(See map on page 54)

General description: Unique, semiprivate clothing-optional oasis in the desert.

Location: About 30 miles west of Pueblo in central southeast Colorado.

Development: Single pool with sun decks and greenhouse lounging area.

Best time to visit: The best time may be winter, when the mild climate and abundant sunshine make this a great place to work on your winter tan.

Restrictions: Clothing-optional and limited membership, but open to visitors.

Access: Accessible by vehicle, but leave large motor homes in town. The route is not well marked but is navigable in all but the muddiest spring weather.

Water temperature: Moderate and variable, from 90 to 100 degrees F.

Services: None. Nearest full services are 10 miles west in Canon City.

Camping: None.

Maps: Florence SE Quadrangle; San Isabel National Forest.

GPS coordinates: N 38 22 09 W 015 02 55.

Finding the springs: From Pueblo, drive west on U.S. Highway 50 to its junction with State Highway 115; drive south, toward Florence, on SH 115 for about 2.5 miles. Turn east, heading toward Portland, on State Highway 120, and after you cross the cattle guard watch for the tall green cactus sign that says Desert Reef Beach Club. Turn right onto County Road 110. From the turn, you will meander through juniper rangeland on gravel roads for about 1.4 miles until you find the DRBC. You will pass a couple of old dwellings, but must watch closely for the very small wooden signs that say only DRBC. Certainly on your first visit to the Desert Reef, you will wonder if you have missed a turnoff somewhere and are about to dead-end in a cow pasture. Be patient, and you will find it. To get there from Colorado Springs, stay south on SH 115 through Penrose, heading toward Florence, and follow the directions above at the turnoff onto SH 120.

Overview: There are some places that are so comfortable and private, it almost seems contrary to share their locations. The Desert Reef Beach Club is just such a place. It is not publicly advertised, and in fact prefers its quiet, subdued anonymity. Just finding the place takes a certain level of determination, for it is only by the most inconspicuous signs that you will be guided to the club's location. At the Rico Café, south of Telluride, I smiled when my waitress replied to my inquiry about Rico Hot Springs. "Yeah, I know about 'em, but if you don't already know, I'm not gonna tell ya." In similar fashion, The Desert Reef Beach Club is well known among the coterie of clothing-optional hot-pool enthusiasts and by the locals who seem to eye the place with a tolerant grin. The regular members of the club, who hail from all over the world and number just over 100, know it to be one of the most relaxing places of its type anywhere.

There are other hot-water developments in this region of south-central Colorado, and most share a common history as to their source of heat. Oil drilling is known for hit-or-miss success, and early in the century when geological mapping and exploration technology was not as sophisticated as it is today, the wells frequently gushed hot water instead of oil. In 1966 the Conoco Huffman well penetrated Precambrian granite at 3,948 feet, but sank to a total depth of 4,240 feet below the surface. If you remember that a mile is about 5,280 feet, you can begin to appreciate the depth of this expensive hole in the ground! The well was plugged at a depth of just over 1,000 feet, and throttled back to an artesian flow of about 300 gallons per minute out of Dakota sandstone, to become the water and heat source for Desert Reef. The water itself has a low sulfur content but is fairly high in calcium. It is mostly the calcium deposits that have been sculpted into a unique and functional backdrop to the main 35-feet-wide by 50-feet-long freeform concrete pool, with a waterfall and niches of mineral formations and potted plants.

The Desert Reef pool is a lovely arrangement, with large concrete sun decks surrounding the pool and a privacy perimeter berm with an eclectic assortment of artwork peeking out of corners and poking up through the sand. L. J. Conrad is co-owner of what used to be an 80-acre homestead, and likely the one who will greet you at the entrance to the DRBC to explain the simple rules of conduct, visitation, and membership. As casual and unique as the Beach Club itself, L. J. will extend a friendly welcome but nevertheless will scrutinize you from beneath his ever-present baseball cap and 1960's free-spirit appearance. You can be sure he is quite adept at estimating your intent and demeanor. Perhaps it is that careful protection of the club and its members that contributes to the sanctity of the oasis that is Desert Reef. The sign on the wall says "Happiness Is No Tan Lines," and that too should give you a clear indication that you are entering an environment where clothing is viewed as an inconvenient social contrivance. If you pass inspection at the front desk, you will notice the small pools of goldfish and oriental Koi that also are pleased the Conoco drillers found hot water and not oil. There is a spacious greenhouse lounge that is heated by the sun as well as hot-water pipes buried beneath the floor. During the days that the DRBC is closed, the facilities are rented out to private functions. The greenhouse has seating and, of course, plants that are being nurtured in their quiet, safe environment, not unlike the club members and their guests. You may also notice a sharp-looking 1961 Corvette in the back, which belongs to L. J. and hints at his colorful nature. The pool is peaceful, idyllic, and clean.

The high (more than 7,000 feet), semidesert aridity of this region of Colorado, known for its "banana belt" climate of nearly continual sunshine, allows the DRBC to be open all year. With about 350 sunny days annually, it is no wonder that so many tanning enthusiasts get brown and relax here. An understated tranquility seems to define this little hideaway, and if you had preconceived notions about naturism or clothing-optional bathing spots, you might be surprised at how easily you melted into the fold here. Enjoying a view of the Wet Mountains on the edge of the beautiful Sangre De Cristo Range while breathing clear, high-elevation air and relaxing in soothing warm water in the uncrowded company of others who understand and appreciate the serenity is perhaps enough to render your preconceptions or conservative ideas unfounded. The regular members of the Desert Reef Beach Club certainly seem to have an enviable ease in their outlook.

Area highlights: The high desert of southern Colorado is full of enticing things to see and do, all year long. Because of the mild climate, winter is not harsh and deep snow is seldom a worry. You are close to the Sangre De Cristo Mountains and on the edge of the San Isabel National Forest, meaning you have enormous outdoor recreational opportunities including fishing, floating, hunting, hiking, rock picking or climbing, mountain biking, and camping. From here you are only an hour's drive away from Colorado Springs and another hour or so from Denver, if the city culture and rhythm is what you enjoy. The area around Canon City is dotted with state and federal prison complexes that seem in harmony with the seclusion that supports so much recreation. You can visit the Prison Museum in Canon City, or the Holy Cross Abbey that houses Benedictine monks. The Arkansas River is known for its whitewater rafting, as is the Royal Gorge Canyon that it carved through the rock over untold millions of years. You can take a scenic railroad trip down into the gorge or view it from the world's highest suspension bridge—about a thousand feet above the river. There are nearby "Fourteeners" like Pikes Peak to the north, if mountain climbing is your pleasure. There is much to see and do, after you have settled your senses at Desert Reef.

SOUTHWEST COLORADO HOT SPRINGS

SW 1

Orvis Hot Springs

General description: Nicely done hot pools and sauna in a low-key setting.
Location: Southwestern Colorado, north of Durango and south of Montrose.
Development: Multiple (indoor and outdoor) pools, sauna, and kitchen facilities.
Best time to visit: Summer is a great time to visit this high-country area.
Restrictions: Stringent rules preclude alcohol and disruptive behavior.
Access: Easy and convenient year-round access by public roads.
Water temperature: Moderate and variable, from 100 to 108 degrees F.
Services: Six lodging rooms. Nearest full services are in Ridgway and Montrose.
Camping: Small camping area, but no hookups provided.
Maps: Dallas Quadrangle; Uncompahgre National Forest; San Juan National Forest.
GPS coordinates: N 38 08 00 W 107 44 02.
Finding the springs: From Montrose, drive south on U.S. Highway 550 about 30 miles to Ridgway. About 1 mile south of Ridgway, take the turnoff to County Road 3, on the west side of the road. Orvis Hot Springs is visible at the turnoff. From Durango, take US 550 north through Ouray to just south of Ridgway, turning west onto CR 3.

Overview: Every hot springs has a flavor of its own. Some are bawdy, raucous, and full of splashing kids. Some are quiet hideaways that take some trouble to get to or even to find. And some, like Orvis Hot Springs, welcome families but still manage to maintain a quiet, subdued privacy while offering enough variety to make everyone happy.

The setting remains fairly undeveloped around Ridgway, which right now is just a small town down the road a short mile, fighting the battle to keep growth at bay or at least under control. The drawing card of this area is its

Orvis Hot Springs, Twin Peaks Motel, Ouray Hot Springs, Box Canyon Hot Springs, Wiesbaden Hot Springs

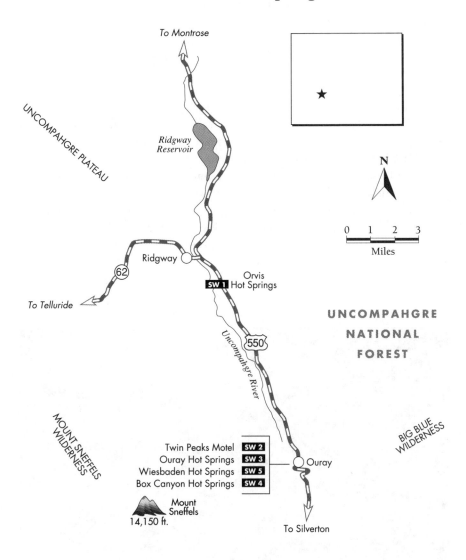

beautiful views of the San Juan Mountains, and the rural western flavor surrounding them. Though there are a few celebrity names like Dennis Weaver and Ralph Lauren linked with property in the area, it is the familiar westward expansion that has been going on since the middle of the nineteenth century that threatens what the locals may value most.

Orvis Hot Springs manager Kim Goodman is a vital part of the flavor of this cozy little resort. Jovial, smiling, and allegorical in his humor, he explains that Orvis was simply a mess not long ago. Since 1987 the location has been a work in progress, and it has been slowly transformed from a farm implement dumping ground to a beautifully landscaped and tastefully furnished spot to relax. In back of the small overnight lodge, which features six guest rooms with access to a community kitchen facility, is the privacy pool, which is kept secluded with a bermed perimeter and a landscaped garden walkway. The large outdoor pool is intentionally kept separate from most of the other facilities, but it still offers exceptional views of the surrounding mountains on the edge of the Uncompahgre Plateau. At about 30 feet in diameter and a little more than 4 feet deep, the pool affords great views and secluded bathing at temperatures of about 104 degrees F. There is a small dry sauna and an adjacent hot pool that is kept near 110 degrees. The grounds have terraced stonework that was added in 1991, and flower gardens fed by warm spring water.

Inside the lodge are private soaking baths done in tile and lovely woodwork, each with a window framing a superb view of the mountains. There is an indoor pool that requires a swimsuit and is beautifully done in wood, glass, tile, and a sprinkling of green plants under the cathedral ceiling. This indoor pool is about 25 feet in diameter, and a refreshing 100 to 102 degrees. It is very nicely done.

Orvis Hot Springs is private and personable.

Historically, as with most hot springs in the area, this water was enjoyed by the natives of the land long before white settlers seized and developed them. The Ute Indians fought for this land, but the battle was never to be won, despite the diplomacy of their famous chief, Ouray. An educated, multilingual man, he tried the diplomatic route to preserve his people's heritage, but preceded their exile with his own death. Lewis Orvis completed a development that became a local gathering site, but eventually the property fell upon hard times—until rescued by Kim Goodman and his fellow "stockholders." Through their savvy and hard work the springs has become an icon for the community. Reassuringly modest and warm with welcome, you will find it difficult not to enjoy your stay here, whether for an afternoon or an entire week.

Area highlights: Located in one of Colorado's most scenic areas, the San Juan Mountains are nothing short of spectacular. Complementing that beauty are boundless opportunities for visitors to enjoy the surroundings here in every season. From hot air balloon rides in nearby Ridgway to fishing on the Ridgway Reservoir, you will enjoy the views. The Uncompahgre Plateau is famous for its hunting and recreational options like hiking, climbing, photography, mountain biking, whitewater rafting, and camping. Nearby is a scenic waterway, the Black Canyon of the Gunnison, and also the Big Blue, Weminuche, and Lizard Head wilderness areas. Just up the road in Ouray is a narrow-gauge railroad that goes to Durango through awesome scenery. There are several old mining ghost towns in the area, and enough four-wheel-drive roads to explore that you could wear out a dozen sets of tires.

In winter, Ouray is an ice-climber's starting point, or you may choose to ice skate in the park. A short drive away, rugged Telluride offers first-class alpine skiing and plenty of snow for cross-country skiers and snowmobilers. Draw a 40-mile-diameter circle to encompass Orvis Hot Springs at the center, and you will find more to do than you will ever have time for.

SW 2

Twin Peaks Motel

(See map on page 61)

General description: Family motel with guest-only pools fed by hot springs.
Location: In southwestern Colorado in the town of Ouray.
Development: Fully equipped motel with three springs-heated pools.
Best time to visit: Summertime is best since they are only open from April to October.
Restrictions: Pools are open only to motel guests.
Access: Easy and convenient year-round access by public roads.
Water temperature: Moderate and variable, from 85 to 105 degrees F.
Services: Full services are available in Ouray.
Camping: None.
Maps: Ouray Quadrangle; San Juan National Forest; Uncompahgre National Forest.
GPS coordinates: N 39 55 56 W 105 16 47.
Finding the springs: In the town of Ouray, southeast of Montrose on U.S. Highway 550 (the main street through town), on the south end of town turn west on Third Avenue and drive for about 1 block. Twin Peaks Motel is on your left.

Overview: In a town that many have described as the Switzerland of Colorado, the Twin Peaks Motel enjoys the Best Western designation, which speaks well of the amenities. They are open six months of the year, from mid-April to mid-October, the height of the tourist season. It is easily one of Colorado's most popular vacation destinations for tourists and residents alike, offering spectacular views of the surrounding San Juan Mountains that tower over the community. Nestled comfortably into the niche left by glacial scouring and the upheavals that gave birth to these exquisite peaks, it is almost as if someone had in mind saving the spot just for Ouray.

There are three pools at the Twin Peaks Motel, a generous-size main pool kept at about 85 degrees F for swimming comfort, and a small rock garden-decorated soaking pool with waterfall that will mellow you out with water near 105 degrees. Indoors you will find a very pretty 60-square-foot blue-tiled whirlpool with great viewing windows—for when the weather is not cooperative enough for you to be outside, lounging on the deck furniture. The outdoor complex has spacious grounds and a play area for children, if you can coax them out of the swimming pool. From just about everywhere, the views of the sheer rock cliffs surround you and the alpine scenery is simply superb. It is difficult to believe sometimes that anyplace can be this pretty. Enjoy a hot soak, followed by a quick cooling dip, and then recline in a poolside lounge chair. You will open your eyes and still be just a little amazed at the beauty around you.

Next door is the Box Canyon Lodge, up the street is the Wiesbaden, and down the road is the Ouray Hot Springs city pool, which testify to the wonderful blessing of hot water this mountain village enjoys. Box Canyon Park is just a block away, and the town of Ouray is as charming and steeped in history as any place could be. Once part of a booming mining town, incredible riches were extracted from the flanks of these mountains. The ore is largely gone, but the lasting value of the hot-springs waters remains. The old buildings in town make for a great walking tour, still reminiscent of the old Victorian style of the day. The Twin Peaks Motel is a great vacation base from which to operate, especially if you have kids and can turn them loose in the outdoor pool. As an added bonus, you can rent a Jeep at the motel and go exploring the back roads and mountain country in all directions. They provide a mapping service to send you out on a fine adventure, but if you prefer, you can take a guided tour.

Either way, those delicious hot springs pools await your return.

Area highlights: Though the Twin Peaks Motel is only open half the year, this is still a vacation paradise all year long. Ice climbing and ice skating in winter are right at your fingertips. Excellent alpine skiing is right around the corner at Telluride, and there are a hundred places to cross-country ski, snowshoe, or snowmobile. In summer there are even more things to do after you have relaxed in the hot pools and enjoyed the area's fine restaurants. You can go hiking, four-wheelin', horseback riding, and mountain biking in those beautiful hills, or see some of the historic mining ghost towns that made Ouray a community in the first place. Take a drive on the Million Dollar Highway and take in some of the most beautiful scenery there is. There are water sports at nearby reservoirs, streams for fishing or kayaking, and national forests for camping or hunting. Chances are you will run out of time or energy before this area gives up its last adventure.

SW 3

Ouray Hot Springs

(See map on page 61)

General description: Large community swimming facility.
Location: Southwestern Colorado to the south of Montrose and north of Durango.
Development: Fully developed fitness center with multiple pools.
Best time to visit: Any time of year is nice, but summer may be best.
Restrictions: None.
Access: Easy and convenient year-round access by public roads.
Water temperature: Moderate and variable, from 78 to 106 degrees F.
Services: Full services are available in Ouray.
Camping: None.
Maps: Ouray Quadrangle; San Juan National Forest; Uncompahgre National Forest.
GPS coordinates: N 38 01 40 W 107 40 15.
Finding the springs: Southeast of Grand Junction, take U.S. Highway 50 toward Gunnison, turning south on U.S. Highway 550 at Montrose. US 550 goes through the middle of Ouray, and the Ouray Hot Springs Pool is on the north end of town, easily visible from the highway. From Durango in the south, take US 550 north through Silverton into Ouray.

Overview: Every so often you will stumble across a place that exceeds all of your expectations. Ouray (pronounced: Yoo-ray) is such a place, and the Hot Springs Pool is the epicenter of a town nestled into a valley that can only be described as gorgeous. Reminiscent of small villages in the Swiss Alps, this community is anchored by the city-owned facility, which is both its social and economic spirit. With a 600-year history of people appreciating the hot springs at Ouray, it is no wonder that life in this small community is centered around those hot waters.

The pool itself is largely fed from water piped out of Box Canyon Hot Springs, but is supplemented by two wells drilled by the city in 1989 at the city park just to the south.

These two shallow (90 feet deep) wells produce the water that feeds directly into the pool. The large perimeter of the pool is oval shaped and sectioned into seven separate areas that vary in water temperature and use. In the temperature range of 97 to 100 degrees F are two shallow (3-feet-deep) sections that together represent about one third of the million gallons of water in the pool—one section is for children and nonswimmers. Pool rules insist that children under 7 years of age must have an adult within reach at all times. There is a 3-feet-deep section on the east end that hovers at around 102 to 106 degrees; it clearly is the most popular location in winter and when nights are cool. The section for small children and nonswimmers holds cooler water—ranging from 78 to 85 degrees—and is slightly deeper (4 feet). The remaining sections are deeper water, from 5 feet to 9 feet in depth, and include a lap section and a diving board area. In this oval, measuring about 150 feet by 250 feet, there should be a temperature and depth to make almost everyone happy.

The facilities at the pool complex include an aerobics and fitness center with weights. There is a spacious bathhouse with hair dryers, playpens for small children, lockers, a snack bar, and a swim shop where you can buy a new suit if you wish. Massages are available, too; this is a nice way to relax aching muscles or relieve stress. You can even rent ice skates in the winter for the rink just up the road. This is a family center, with lots of room for everyone and a delightful feeling of community throughout. The clear, clean water is very low in sulfur, but stoked with minerals, making it a sought-after therapeutic pleasure for many "hot-potters."

Although the pool complex is beautifully done, a big part of what makes it special is the spectacular views in every direction. Steep, rugged, and high, the San Juan Mountains rise up close at hand in red-rock canyons and soaring cliffs. You are surrounded by majestic heights that frame incredible nighttime vistas of the constellations through the mist rising around you. When the moon is full and there is snow on the ground, the pool stays open later than usual in recognition of the beautiful lunar spectacle, the moonlight scattering off canyon walls and glowing white peaks.

Historically the town of Ouray, named for the Uncompahgre Ute Indian chief, has a colorful background. When miners Gus Begole and Jack Echols came up from Silverton in 1875 and found both silver and gold, the rush was on to find riches in the hills. They established the Mineral Farm claim about a mile from town, but made the mistake of telling others about their discoveries. The area became a boomtown whose wealth and beauty attracted permanent settlers, some of whom built impressive Victorian-style buildings that still stand. By the late 1800s, the town was bustling with saloons, brothels, and a growing number of more permanent developments, but the abandonment of the silver standard for U.S. currency altered some of Ouray's hustle. Still, the Camp Bird Mine owned by Thomas Walsh produced millions of dollars in gold, back when a million dollars was a *lot* of money. Sold for $5.2 million in 1902, the Camp Bird Mine was legendary. Walsh and his family were owners of the Hope Diamond and the social stature brought by wealth at that level.

In 1920 Ouray Hot Springs was called Radium Hot Springs, but by 1925 the Ouray Recreation Association Corporation was established to formalize development of the springs. Built with volunteer labor, the pool opened in

1926 and was followed a year later by the bathhouse. Four years after that, the association turned the pool over to the City of Ouray, and it continues to provide funding for itself and other city parks.

Named in the National Register of Historic Places, Ouray Hot Springs is very much a community focal point. Remnants of the mines still exist, and many of the grand old buildings of the mining era still add charm to the town, but Ouray's lasting wealth may be the hot water that has flowed for centuries and will continue for centuries more.

Area highlights: This is a stunningly beautiful area. The San Juan Mountains are some of Colorado's most picturesque. They not only provide the backdrop for Ouray Hot Springs, but they also provide countless opportunities to enjoy their beauty all year long. The narrow-gauge railroad that runs from Durango to Ouray is a scenic delight, as is the famous Million Dollar Highway, named as the most scenic 70-mile drive in all of Colorado. There are challenging four-wheel-drive roads that traverse high passes from Silverton to Ouray and lead to places like the Camp Bird Mine. The San Juan range is a paradise for hikers, hunters, anglers, wildlife viewers, and photographers. There are old mining ghost towns in every corner of this area, giving you a glimpse of the not-so-distant past.

In spring there is rushing water everywhere, offering whitewater rafting, kayaking, and fishing. In summer there are endless trails to explore on foot, on horseback, or by ATV or four-wheel-drive vehicle; and there is scenic camping and great mountain biking to be experienced. You can hunt in autumn or photograph a countryside emblazoned with color. Telluride ski area is an hour away for winter skiing, and ice climbing or skating is close at hand.

As a summer-centric vacation town, Ouray is well equipped to rent, loan, or sell whatever equipment you might need to enjoy their locale. They know you will return to enjoy the pride of their community—the Ouray Hot Springs Pool.

SW 4

Box Canyon Hot Springs

(See map on page 61)

General description: This is a fully developed motel featuring springs-fed redwood tubs as part of the guest-only facilities.

Location: About 40 miles south of Montrose in Ouray, in southwestern Colorado.

Development: Developed lodge with hot tubs.

Best time to visit: Hot tubs are great in the winter, but area recreational opportunities are probably best in summer.

Restrictions: Hot Tubs are only for guests of the lodge.

Access: Easy and convenient year-round access by public roads.

Water temperature: Moderate and variable, from 103 to 108 degrees F.

Services: Overnight accommodations for lodge guests and all services in Ouray.

Camping: None.

Maps: Ouray Quadrangle; San Juan National Forest; Uncompahgre National Forest.

GPS coordinates: N 38 01 25 W 107 40 27.

Finding the springs: Southeast of Grand Junction, take U.S. Highway 50 toward Gunnison, turning south on U.S. Highway 550 at Montrose. US 550 goes through the middle of Ouray, and the Box Canyon Lodge is on the south side of town only two blocks from the main road, on Third Avenue. From Durango to the south, take US 50 north through Silverton into Ouray.

Overview: The Box Canyon Lodge and Hot Springs is situated in one of Colorado's most uniquely beautiful settings. The small town of Ouray (pronounced Yoo-ray) nestles in a lofty valley (7,800 feet in elevation) with spectacular mountain vistas in every direction. Like a little slice of Switzerland, the area is bursting with charm and the sheer beauty of the San Juan range towering above and all around. The folks running the motel even seem blessed with the exceedingly pleasant manner you would find in a small village in the Swiss Alps. A motel with hot tubs for its guests may have a different perspective on natural hot springs than a wilderness hike-in location, but this very civilized use of nature's geothermal energy is nothing but comfortable. The lodge is in town, but far enough from the main road to avoid much of the noise. It is still an easy walk to many of this quaint little burg's restaurants and shops. Four redwood hot tubs fed by the hot springs terrace the hillside behind the lodge with connecting decks, taking good advantage of the panoramic views. The hot-springs water is also used in conjunction with a heat exchanger to warm domestic water and provide space heating for the lodge.

The management of the Box Canyon Lodge makes it clear that they place an emphasis upon providing a peaceful, relaxing environment, and discourage disruptive behavior. This is not a cut-rate accommodation where you can get away with bringing your mountain bike and your dog into the room with you. In fact, there is a $100 fine added to your bill if they catch you sneaking your pet into the room! If you have a van full of noisy children, this may not be your best choice for a stay, but if you are looking for a relaxing place to land after spending the day skiing at nearby Telluride or hiking the majestic San Juans, you will be hard pressed to do much better.

There is an interesting history to consider as you soak your bones in low-sulfur water, kept near the hot-tub optimum 104 degrees F amid the splendor of those impressive mountains. Like most of the thermal springs that dot this area of southern Colorado, there is a rich background dating back far before the European settlements. The Ute Indians, after whose charismatic but controversial Chief Ouray the town was named, were known to have been frequent visitors before the first trappers and prospectors moved into the area. As you steep in the deep, cask-type tub and fizz to the hydro jets, consider that more than a hundred years ago this charming village was once called Uncompahgre City, before becoming incorporated in honor of Chief Ouray during the American centennial year of 1876. Gold and silver prospectors Gus Begole and Jack Echols found easy pickings here after coming up from Silverton. Their Mineral Farm claim started a stampede that resulted in more than 400 new residents in only one year's time. In 10 years the bustling little mining town had tripled to over 1,200 and soon boasted a school, churches, and restaurants, as well as assorted bars and brothels. It is an amusing irony that prospectors who found wealth soon drew crowds, which in turn brought dance halls and houses of ill repute with churches following quickly behind. Was the style of life back then to dig a day's wages in gold, spend it on supper and whiskey at the saloon, visit the bordello, and then do it all again the next day until your claim dried up? Would you then seek new promise in another high-mountain canyon? Though the prospectors may have begun the immigration to Ouray, folks of less-transient view found it worth staying.

As you sink deeper into the frothy hot water in your tub after dark, look down to the twinkle of lights below you and know that this whole community is included in the National Register of Historic Districts. Much of the Victorian style and substance remains with buildings that were largely completed between 1880 and 1900, blended with a unique flavoring of American West and European chalet-style mountain décor. The cosmopolitan charm is hard

Hillside Hot Tubs at Box Canyon Lodge.

not to enjoy, especially from the sanctity of your private tub and surrounding deck. There is room in the tub for three of your friends to join you, but because Box Canyon Lodge has stepped the decks and tubs up the hillside, you have a surprisingly private little world in which to relax. At night or in the winter when snow changes the way everything looks, there are mystical sensations that perhaps come from the water, which once warmed Indian chiefs and the muscles of tired miners.

In 1925 Bessi and Richard Cogar owned the land upon which Box Canyon Hot Springs bubbles its water at temperatures above 140 degrees F. They built an exclusive sanitarium based on the restorative powers of the water, but it may have been the exclusive and spectacularly scenic location that made this such a popular destination. Four years later the Cogar Sanitarium was sold to Charles Kent, from Peoria Illinois, who renamed it the Sweet Skin Sanitarium. The property continued to evolve through an assortment of owners and developed into the lodge that rests on part of the Cogars' original acreage.

The brothels have disappeared and mining is no longer the center of economic and social life, but a great deal of the old town is still there. A short walk through town will take you back into history with very little imagination required.

The Box Canyon Lodge, with its hillside wooden hot pots, is a comfortably modern facility tucked into the vest pocket of a town with enormous character and a colorful legacy. Embraced in the fold of truly beautiful mountains, you may find it difficult to leave this place.

Area highlights: This is a mecca, not just for those seeking the warmth of several hot springs in which to soak, but for almost every conceivable outdoor recreation. It is a year-round feast of opportunity in some of the most beautiful scenery anywhere. The narrow-gauge railroad that runs from Durango to Ouray is a scenic delight, as is the famous Million Dollar Highway, named as the most scenic 70-mile drive in all of Colorado. There are also some wonderful four-wheel-drive roads that traverse high passes from Silverton to Ouray. The San Juan range is not only awesome in its beauty, but is a wildlife paradise for hunters, anglers, and photographers.

There are old mining ghost towns in every corner of this area, and they are vibrant fodder for the imagination. In Ouray, the Camp Bird Mine produced enough gold to make the Thomas Walsh family extremely wealthy, so much so that daughter Evalyn Walsh McLean bought the Hope Diamond. In Telluride lives the history of Diamond Tooth Leona and Jew Fanny who, among their sister ladies of the evening, worked 26 cribs and parlor houses such as the Whitehouse and Senate. At one point, Telluride (named for the element tellurium, which is often attached to silver and gold ore) harbored 175 prostitutes on the south side of Colorado Avenue—the red light district. Parson Hogg's first church services were held in a Telluride tavern, if that helps you understand the culture of the day. The Ophir and Silverton ghost towns are no more than abandoned relics of bygone days when men grew fabulously wealthy and desperately poor, side by side.

Mesa Verde National Park is home to some of the cliff dwellings of the prehistoric Anasazi Indians. The Black Canyon of the Gunnison brings the Grand Canyon to mind, and offers fine fishing, whitewater rafting, and scenic hiking. Colorado National Monument is a display of sandstone pillar and cavern formations, while in the vicinity of Grand Junction is Dinosaur Valley, where the infamous tyrannosaurus and gentle brontosaurus once roamed.

In winter, world-class Telluride Ski Area is only a 1-hour drive away, and right in Ouray is the variety and quality of ice-climbing that has earned it the title of Ice-Climbing Capitol of North America. There is even a public ice-skating park on the north end of town near Ouray. Whether you want to rent a Jeep, a snowboard, a horse, a hot air balloon, a mountain bike, or a whitewater raft, you will run out of time long before you run out of exciting things to do with The Box Canyon Lodge as your home base.

Box Canyon Falls, which as you might guess is the namesake of the lodge, is a city park just a quick stroll away (one block to the west). There you will find a wooden boardwalk with safety fencing pinned to the sheer rock walls through which the torrent of water pours that carved out the canyon. The falls and the steep black rock canyon walls make for a worthwhile visit.

SW 5

Wiesbaden Hot Springs

(See map on page 61)

General description: A tastefully done lodge with indoor and outdoor pools.

Location: Southwest Colorado—south of Montrose and north of Durango in Ouray.

Development: Underground hot vapor caves, outdoor pools, and comfortable lodge.

Best times to visit: Any season—but very busy on holidays.

Restrictions: No smoking, no pets, and no children under five in the pools.

Access: Easy and convenient year-round access by public roads.

Water temperature: Moderate and variable, from 100 to 110 degrees F.

Services: Full services in Ouray.

Camping: None.

Maps: Ouray Quadrangle; San Juan National Forest; Uncompahgre National Forest.

GPS coordinates: N 38 01 16 W 107 40 03.

Finding the springs: Southeast of Grand Junction, take U.S. Highway 50 toward Gunnison, turning south on U.S. Highway 550 at Montrose. US 550 goes through the middle of Ouray, and the Wiesbaden Spa and Lodge is three blocks east of the main road on Sixth Avenue. From Durango to the south, take US 50 north through Silverton into Ouray.

Overview: Casual and elegant. Although the words seem almost contradictory, they aptly describe this charming lodge and hot-springs spa. Decorated with an eye for style and a European flavor, Wiesbaden Hot Springs is a memorable inn with outstanding views of the spectacular San Juan Mountains that enshrine the village of Ouray. Linda Wright-Minter is the latest in a long history of owners, dating back to 1832 when A. G. Dunbar first discovered a 40-barrel-per-hour flow of hot water in the process of building his house on the site. The atmosphere is refreshingly subdued with an aura of respect for tranquility and the spiritual history of centuries past.

On the site of what was the first hot springs used for commercial purposes in Ouray County, the Wiesbaden (properly pronounced Vees-bodden, given its German derivation) was a serendipitous discovery by Dunbar, who was at the time the Ouray postmaster and apothecary. The first building constructed at the springs was a simple 12-feet by 24-feet rectangle named Dunbar's Plunge Bathhouse, which quickly became popular with local miners and townsfolk.

Wiesbaden Hot Springs offers a taste of Europe in the Rockies.

Dunbar dreamed of expanding his business, and bought another site to which he piped his hot water. The new structure was a two-story enterprise with eight windows, to brighten the feel of the natatorium. With the coming national depression, Dunbar's heavily leveraged properties defaulted on their loans and led to a trustees' sale in Denver, where they were sold for $5,000. Promptly sold again to John McCloud, the larger of the developments became the Ouray Mineral Hot Springs, with a new emphasis on health instead of recreation. Advertisements heralded the greatest amount of radiation in any hot-springs waters, although it is doubtful any reliable evidence existed to support those grand claims. Up the hill at the original site, there was an enterprise named Mother Buchanan's Bathhouse. Some speculation between the lines of history points fingers at "Mother" being more appropriately called "Madam," but in those bawdy times of mining and feast-or-famine settlements, the distinction may be irrelevant. Certainly Ouray was a colorful place to be in that era.

In 1926 the properties were sold to Dr. Charles V. Bates, whose vision was to build a combination sanitarium and hospital. What was once the Bates Hospital (he called it The Radium Vapor Health Institute upon its completion in 1929) is now the Ouray County Historical Museum, and Dunbar's springs have become the Wiesbaden Hot Springs Spa and Lodge. It was Bates who excavated the vapor caves and ran the hospital for nearly 20 years. Briefly named Spa Lopa and then purchased in 1971 by the Zimmers, the site is now under the management of Wright-Minter and comfortably ensconced in its reputation as a relaxing enclave of civility and good taste in a truly beautiful setting.

When you enter the lobby of the lodge you are greeted with warmth that comes from cathedral ceilings, skylights, natural wood, expansive glass, and a bounty of green plants.

From the deck of the crystal-clear outdoor pool (which ranges from 100 to 103 degrees F), the view of the surrounding mountains is simply inspirational. There is an enclosed outdoor private pool with its own springfall called the Lorelei, available at an extra charge unless the main pool is being cleaned, when it becomes available to guests for no added fees. Its name is an interesting reference to the German heritage again, with the legend of the siren Lorelei whose beauty and singing enticed sailors to wreck upon the reefs below her rock above the Rhine River. Downstairs you will find the vapor caves, a dressing area, workout room, and a lounge and relaxation area with fresh water and an ice machine. The soaking pool water cascades over a rock wall at nearly 110 degrees F. The ambiance is subdued, quiet, and cleansing for the mind and body.

A full range of therapeutic massage is available to guests including Swedish, sports, and acupressure treatments. You can enjoy an aromatherapy wrap or a deep-cleaning facial, too. With the restrictions on rowdy behavior and no allowance for small children in the pools, the emphasis is on peace and quiet. Above ground in the main pool, you still will not find a municipal pool environment, which is left to the Ouray Hot Springs Pool that is owned by the city. Rather, you will experience a more adult sanctuary where you can reflect on the history and the lasting beauty that surrounds you. The Wiesbaden Hot Springs is very nicely done.

Area highlights: In one of Colorado's most scenic areas, the San Juan Mountains give ample opportunity to enjoy the surroundings in every season. The Uncompahgre Plateau is famous for its hunting and other recreational options like hiking, climbing, photography, mountain biking, whitewater rafting, and camping. Nearby is the scenic waterway, the Black Canyon of the Gunnison, and also the Big Blue, Weminuche, and Lizard Head wilderness areas. Just up the road in Ouray is a narrow-gauge railroad that goes to Durango through spectacular and remote scenery. There also is a fine selection of other hot springs, if you are an impassioned hot-potter. There are several old mining ghost towns with a rich and varied history, and more four-wheel-drive roads to explore than a dozen summer vacations will find.

In winter, Ouray is an ice-climbing center, or you may choose to ice skate in the park. A short drive away, rugged Telluride Ski Area offers first-class alpine skiing and plenty of snow for cross-country skiers, snowmobilers, and snowshoe hikers.

SW 6

Trimble Hot Springs

General description: Community resort pool and soaking spa.

Location: In southwest Colorado 6 miles north of Durango.

Development: Tastefully done large swimming pool, hot pools, and picnic area.

Best times to visit: Easy access all year, but it may be best from spring through fall.

Restrictions: None. Open to the public.

Access: Easy and convenient year-round access on public roads.

Water temperature: Moderate and variable, from 85 to 108 degrees F.

Services: Full services available nearby in Durango.

Camping: None.

Maps: Hermosa Quadrangle; San Juan National Forest.

GPS coordinates: N 37 23 27 W 107 50 52.

Finding the springs: From Durango, drive north on the scenic byway U.S. Highway 550 for about 6.5 miles, and look for the Trimble Hot Springs sign on your left. Trimble is about 50 yards ahead. You can see the building from the road. From Grand Junction, take U.S. Highway 50 south to Delta and US 550 almost to Durango. Trimble Hot Springs is across the road from the Dalton Ranch Golf Club, about 6.5 miles due north of Durango.

Overview: Now one of Colorado's most pleasant community-flavored hot-springs pools, Trimble has seen some dramatic changes in its varied existence. As with most of the thermal springs of the southwest, this one was discovered and enjoyed by Native Americans long before the European settlers arrived to wrest away control. We will never know just how much history preceded the arrival of Frank Trimble, for whom the springs are named, in 1874, but you can gain insight by knowing that in the cliffs above the pools are the inaccessible ruins of the ancient Anasazi Indians. There are Anasazi sites in nearby canyons, and of course in Mesa Verde National Park, if that history piques your cultural curiosity.

Of more current interest is the beautiful little oasis that is Trimble Hot Springs. It is as tidy and eminently presentable as any community could hope for a private commercial operation to be. There is a large 85-degree-F, Olympic-size pool that is just right for a town like Durango to happily amuse an entire squadron of its children on a warm summer afternoon. Next to that, and delightfully shaded by large trees, is a pair of therapy pools whose temperatures tickle the thermometer at 102 and 108 degrees, respectively. There also is an outdoor whirlpool tub at 104 degrees. The main building features a small aerobic

Trimble Hot Springs

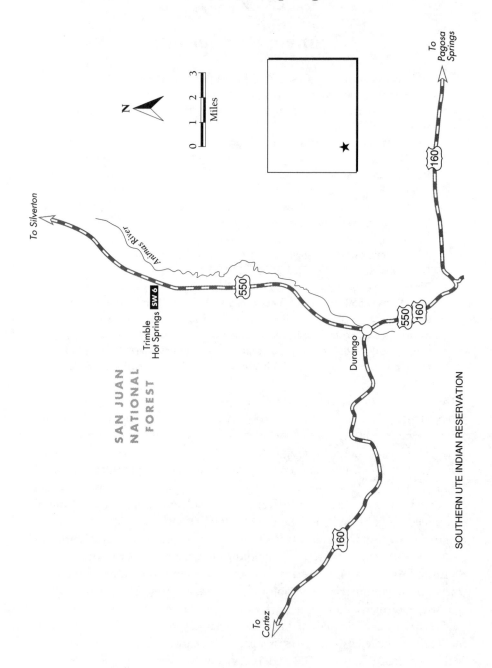

workout room, a snack bar, and the Red Rock Room, which is available for small conferences and wedding parties. You can get an herbal body wrap or any of an assortment of massage therapies, some in combination with a hot soak. You can even arrange to receive swimming lessons in the shadow of the beautiful rock cliffs.

The memorable thing about Trimble Hot Springs is how nicely everything is arranged. In all but the winter months, trees and grass make an idyllic setting relaxing, even when the large pool is full of raucous youngsters enjoying themselves. There is room for a picnic lunch near the barbecue, and plenty of well-kept greenery to make you feel like it is a garden party with a great view of the San Juan Mountains. The bathhouse and grounds are clean and tidy. What a nice spot. It is the kind of place I would be happy to take my youngsters for a family afternoon of relaxation (for me) and fun (for them).

The history of Trimble Hot Springs has some high spots and some low spots. Owner and former ski racer Reudi Bear considers himself a caretaker of a natural wonder that was once trashed and buried by mud and debris. Since 1979, when he took over his caretaking duties, the place has been dramatically transformed. Once the site of hotels, one of them an elegant building called the Hermosa Hotel, owned by cattle baron T. D. Burns, all of them were razed by fire, so common before electrical code safety standards and fire departments. An assortment of rogues and luminaries visited over the years when it was a "social house" with exotic dancers of great imagination. It finally collapsed into decay before its rebirth under Reudi. Soaking in the warm, wispy thermals of the warmest therapy pool, it is interesting to consider the variety of life the water flowing from the hot springs has fed over untold generations. It was a warm watering hole for animals before humans arrived, hallowed ground for the Anasazi, a bawdy social center during the early settlement of the American West; and finally, today it is a peaceful and happy community development that seems like the one to model upon if you could design your own.

Area highlights: The name *Durango* has a western, John Wayne ring to it, and the town has a familiar look from all the Hollywood movies filmed there. There is much that colors this area with western heritage, from the mining history in the north near Silverton to the southwestern Native American culture. The San Juan National Forest beckons with outdoor recreation for everyone. There is hunting, fishing, biking, and hiking among these rugged peaks. Just up the road is Purgatory Ski Area, and a bit farther still is Telluride. Consider a snowmobile tour in the high country, a horse-drawn sleigh ride, or a journey on the scenic Durango and Silverton winter train. Mesa Verde National Park displays the Anasazi ruins and anthropological history at Cliff Palace, while nearby Cortez is known as the archaeological center of the United States. The Ute Mountain Tribal Park preserves remnants of the ancient Puebloan culture. Hovenweep (a Ute word meaning "deserted valley") National Monument guards ruins dating back hundreds of years. If you like gaming, Ute Mountain Casino may be worth a visit. The San Juan Skyway is a scenic drive from Mancos to Cortez and up State Highway 145 to Telluride that is full of spectacular 14,000-feet-high mountains, rugged red-rock canyons, and beautiful high country. Numerous reservoirs and rivers like the Mancos, Dolores, Animas, and Piedra offer floating, boating, and fishing. There are music festivals, arts and crafts fairs, hot air balloon rallies, golf tourneys, raft races, foot races, and rodeos in Cortez, Durango, and Mancos. Any time of year, there is much to do.

SW 7

Rainbow Hot Springs

General description: Moderate hike to small streamside pool in wilderness.
Location: South-central Colorado in Weminuche Wilderness near Pagosa Springs.
Development: Undeveloped except for rocks piled to make a pool below springs.
Best times to visit: Summer and early fall are best because of access.
Restrictions: Wilderness area—no mechanized transport or motors.
Access: Easy and convenient public access to trailhead, but private property and wilderness rules apply thereafter. Access may be difficult in winter.
Water temperature: Moderate and variable, averaging about 103 degrees F; pool varies by season.
Services: Pagosa Springs has nearest full services, about 25 miles from trailhead.
Camping: Camping in primitive area only—no vehicle access to hot springs.
Maps: South River Peak Quadrangle; San Juan National Forest; Rio Grande National Forest.
GPS coordinates: N 37 30 33 W 106 52 28.

Finding the springs: From Pagosa Springs in the far south of Colorado, take U.S. Highway 160 about 18 miles northeast, toward Wolf Creek Pass. Just about a half mile past the Archuleta and Mineral county line, look for the West Fork Campground Road on your left (west side of the road) as you begin to ascend the pass. It is less than 4 miles to the trailhead, and clearly marked by signs. Coming from Wolf Creek Pass, you will feel as if you are not completely on level ground yet when the West Fork (of the San Juan River) Campground comes up on your right. If you cross the Archuleta-Mineral county line, you have gone too far!

The hike in is about 4.5 miles each way. Private property for the first mile is heavily posted, almost to the wilderness boundary. Trail junctions can be somewhat unclear after crossing into the wilderness, but when in doubt, take the trail to your left going in. It will probably be the trail most heavily used. Be sure to stay to the left when you see the Beaver Creek Trail (no. 560) on the right; at this point you are not far from the springs. Rainbow is not marked, but when you come to an obvious camping area among mature trees with the river on your left, look for the pool next to the river, 40 feet down an embankment. If you cross into semi-open meadow, after reaching the heavily used camping area, you have gone too far and must go back to look for the spring immediately adjacent to the river. Take a topographical map along.

Rainbow Hot Springs, The Spring Inn, The Spa

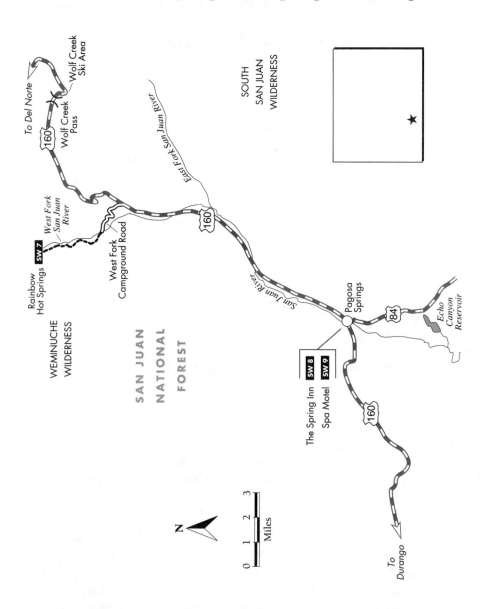

Overview: This is not exactly a hidden, secret hot springs, but it is not as easy as driving up with your beach towel in hand and going in for a dip, either. The first consideration is the hike from the trailhead. It's about 4.5 miles in from the trailhead. The first 500 yards is probably the toughest part of the trail, so don't give up too soon! The first mile is heavily posted with signs indicating private property and Rainbow Trail signs with red arrows pointing the way. Shortly thereafter, you will cross into the Weminuche Wilderness, and the trail follows the West Fork of the San Juan River, beside which the hot spring nestles.

While angling steadily uphill for most of the hike, the trail is generally quite gradual, and to my way of thinking this is a very moderate hike. I ambled along beside river escarpment views and through aspen groves and plantations of skunk cabbage, taking about an hour and a half to get to the springs during the first week of July in 1998. There are assorted creek crossings along the way, but any water flow of substance has a stout wooden bridge to keep your feet dry. That's a change from years past, before the bridges were built, when it took determination and wading skill to ford high runoff streams. There are beautiful rocky vistas that peek through the trees from time to time in the direction of Wolf Creek Pass, and many places along the way you will walk beside the rushing, noisy river. Most of the trail winds through timbered hillsides with many stream rivulets and mature trees measuring up to 4 feet in diameter at the base. It's a relaxing, enjoyable hike if you are in good condition.

If you do not exercise regularly at high elevation, or if you are packing a heavy load, the hike may be a bit more daunting, so plan on extra time to get there and back comfortably.

Rainbow Hot Springs spouts from a crease in the solid rock about 15 feet above the West Fork of the San Juan River, cascading into a small foot-soaking pool fashioned from log and rock by busy hands, and then falls into the main pool below. The big pool shares a short, stacked-rock wall with the river on one side and the soaking pool on the other. The soaking pool is about 15 feet by 6 feet, and perhaps 3 feet deep at its deepest point. It is a delicious temperature for soaking in summertime, and just big enough to hold two or three people in comfort—more if they are already good friends. The beauty of the hot springs is its secluded location and riverside location. You can become warm from your soak, splash in the cold river for a heart-thumping moment, and then leap back into the soothing warmth. No sleepy nerve cells after that! From your protected river hot pot you can enjoy crisp, fresh air and green trees all around you, with the roaring stream filling your ears with water music.

The springs access is good enough that you will have to plan carefully to have the luxury of a private pool. Although during my last visit I had the place to myself all afternoon, I did bump into several hikers as I was headed down the trail. The camping area above the pool is obviously well used, and speaks of potentially crowded conditions on weekends or holidays during July and August. The elevation is high enough in the mountains that you need to keep an eye on the weather, because it can change abruptly. Study the satellite maps to make sure you have clear weather ahead, go early on a nonholiday weekday, and

Rainbow Hot Springs is well worth the hike.

you may well enjoy this beautiful wilderness retreat in solitude. It is one of Colorado's prettiest.

Area highlights: The Pagosa Springs area of southern Colorado is increasingly popular. Part of the reason for its popularity is the boundless opportunity for outdoor recreation.

The town of South Fork on the east side of Wolf Creek Pass is evidently popular with Texans in the summer months, as there may seem to be more Texas plates than Colorado plates. Winter weather is a haven for skiers, who abound here, due to nearly 40 feet of annual snowfall. Every facet of winter sport from ice-climbing to snowmobiling is possible. For a really special excursion, board the Cumbres and Toltec Scenic Railroad in either Chama, New Mexico or Antonito, Colorado and ride through 64 miles of spectacular scenery. The Durango-Silverton railroad is similar in its traverse of superb scenery. West of Durango is the Ute Mountain Tribal Park and the Mesa Verde National Park, where you can see ancient cliff dwellings and Anasazi ruins; or you can view the same even closer in the Chimney Rock Archaeological Area. Colorado's largest wilderness area, the Weminuche Wilderness, and also the South San Juan or La Garita wilderness areas offer exceptional hiking, hunting, camping, rafting, horse trails, wildlife viewing, and photography. The headwaters of the Rio Grande provide entertainment for anglers and rafters. In Pagosa Springs there is an annual Folk Festival over the Labor Day weekend, and a 27-hole championship golf course and tennis complex near town can help keep you entertained. Every season of the year is a picnic of activity and recreational opportunity.

SW 8

The Spring Inn at Pagosa Springs

(See map on page 82)

General description: Recently developed collection of hot pools alongside the river.

Location: Southwestern Colorado in the town of Pagosa Springs.

Development: Eleven assorted sizes and shapes of small hot-pool settings.

Best times to visit: Summer evenings are cool, but days can be hot. This is a great place to visit in winter after a day of skiing at nearby Wolf Creek Ski Area.

Restrictions: None.

Access: Easy and convenient year-round access by public roads.

Water temperature: Moderate and variable, from 94 to 111 degrees F.

Services: Full services are available in Pagosa Springs.

Camping: None. Limited recreational-vehicle parking on site—no hook-ups.

Maps: Pagosa Springs Quadrangle; San Juan National Forest; Rio Grande National Forest.

GPS coordinates: N 37 15 52 W 107 00 37.

Finding the springs: From Durango, drive east on U.S. Highway 160 to the middle of Pagosa Springs and turn south at the (only) stoplight, onto Hot Springs Boulevard. Just across the river bridge immediately on your right is The Spring Inn. From Alamosa, drive west on US 160 and look for the stoplight in Pagosa Springs; turn south onto Hot Springs Boulevard. The Spring Inn is easily visible from the road.

Overview: If variety is the spice of life, this is one zesty spot. Situated near the center of Pagosa Springs and alongside the San Juan River, the springs at The Spring Inn are a collection of eleven individually designed pools that use the therapeutic water from the Great Pagosa Aquifer. With names like The Waterfall, The Lobster Pot, and Sunset Social Club, you can imagine that each has its own personality. The large central pool features a submerged boardwalk and rope-railing crossing. There is an ancient fountainhead of mineral tufa bubbling water above the garden of pools down to the river, connected by stone walkways and paths amid gardens, lily pads, and fishponds. With such an artistic collection of small pools that vary in size, temperature, and view of the river, everyone should be able to find his or her perfect zone.

In the days when the Ute Indian population was prevalent, the Great Pagosa Springs were a spiritual and cultural center that they believed to be a

The Spring Inn offers history and variety. PHOTO COURTESY OF THE SPRING INN

source of power to those who partook of the mineral-laden waters. With the onerous takeover of the area by the white settlers, the therapeutic value of the water has evolved through a range from aversion to worship. Eventually the springs saw development and exploitation that allows some of the municipal buildings in Pagosa Springs to be heated by the water, as is The Spring Inn.

During the middle and late 1800s there were many treaty violations between the Native Americans and the white settlers, with conflicts mediated by the U.S. Cavalry, inevitably to the detriment of the Utes. It is a sad and conflicted time in our history to which we can devote thought as we peacefully soak in the hot pools whose water gave vitality and spiritual energy to the Ute Indians centuries ago.

The facilities at The Spring Inn include lounging decks; a clean, efficient bathhouse with lockers; and a range of rejuvenative treatments administered by 10 massage therapists, a chiropractor, and an acupuncturist. Between the soothing mineral waters and the professional services, all your aches and pains should be assuaged in short order. Just the pleasure of the streamside hot pots should be great therapy for a stressed mind. The springs are open to the public, but management discourages anything less than well supervised children, and disruptive behavior by anyone is not tolerated

Just a short stroll to the southwest is the site of the original Great Pagosa Hot Springs, which is fenced for safety and preservation of the site. There are four storyboards built by the city of Pagosa Springs that detail information about the springs. The history of the Great Pagosa Hot Springs, the geologic requirements for a hot springs, the stratigraphic section at the springs, and the distribution of the geothermal heating system are explained in easy-to-understand graphics and text. It is accurate and an excellent way to gain a better understanding of this area and hot springs in general. This is an interesting place.

Area highlights: The sporting goods store across the street is an indicator of some of the adventures waiting for you in the surrounds of Pagosa Springs. Juan's Sports is located adjacent to The Spring Inn, and rents skis, snowboards, mountains bikes, and kayaks. This is a great place to explore rivers like the San Juan or Piedra by kayak, raft, canoe, or drift boat while fishing or just soaking up the scenery. If you prefer larger bodies of water for water skiing, angling, or sailing, the nearby Navajo or Vellecito reservoirs will suit you, as will an assortment of smaller lakes south and west of Pagosa Springs. The South San Juan and Weminuche wilderness areas are gorgeous, and reward hikers, photographers, and explorers with beautiful scenery for camping, fishing, and hunting. The San Juan and Rio Grande national forests are a bounty of outdoor opportunity. If your pleasure is history and native cultures, you will enjoy seeing the Southern Ute Indian Reservation, Chimney Rock Archeological Area, and the Anasazi ruins at Mesa Verde. The Durango and Silverton and Cumbres and Toltec scenic railroads attract tourists from all over the country with their spectacular scenic routes. In summer you may choose simply to relax on the championship 27-hole golf course in Pagosa Springs. If winter sports are your interest, consider Purgatory and Wolf Mountain ski areas, with some of the heaviest annual snowfalls in all of Colorado, or boundless snowmobiling, cross-country skiing, and snowshoe hiking in the national forests.

You might live a lifetime in this area and never see half of what it offers.

SW 9

The Spa at Pagosa Springs

(See map on page 82)

General description: Motel and recreational-vehicle facility with hot springs pools and baths.

Location: South-central Colorado in Pagosa Springs, east of Durango.

Development: Hot springs pools, steam room, motel and recreational-vehicle park.

Best times to visit: Spring, summer, and fall are the most enjoyable.

Restrictions: None.

Access: Easy and convenient year-round access by public roads.

Water temperature: Moderate and seasonally variable, from 85 to 108 degrees F.

Services: Full services are available in Pagosa Springs.

Camping: Yes—full recreational-vehicle hookups, pull-through, and cable TV.

Maps: Pagosa Springs Quadrangle; San Juan National Forest; Rio Grande National Forest.

GPS coordinates: N 37 15 55 W 107 00 35.

Finding the springs: From Durango, drive east on U.S. Highway 160 to the middle of town and turn south at the (only) stoplight, onto Hot Springs Boulevard. Just across the river bridge, three blocks farther on your left, is the spa. From Alamosa, drive west on US 160 and look for the stoplight, turning south onto Hot Springs Boulevard. The Spa at Pagosa Springs is easily visible from Hot Springs Boulevard.

Overview: A dynasty of family ownership has defined the Spa at Pagosa Springs for more than 40 years, and it has earned its place in the community after growing up with Pagosa Springs. Long ago, the native Ute and Navajo Indians favored this location as a spiritual healing place, and a neutral zone was shared without confrontation. The Pagosa Springs Chamber of Commerce loosely translates the Ute word "Pahgosa" to mean "healing waters," but it seems a more accurate interpretation points to "boiling waters." In the Ute tribal tongue, "Pah" means *water* and "gosa" means *boiling*. There is a significant amount of sulfur and mineral content in this unusually hot springs (said to be the hottest in all of Colorado), but to many hot springs disciples, that is a therapeutic asset rather than a deficit. A number of people throughout history have touted the healthful benefits of this and other mineral springs, while lacking specific scientific evidence to support the belief. You may not see any published guarantees testifying to the health benefits. The native Indians attributed great healing powers to the mineral springs, and newspaper testimonials in the late 1800s said that everything from venereal disease to paralysis was cured by their waters. Indeed, one thing is certain: The aroma is reliable and distinctive.

There are a number of options available to visitors to the spa, among them being the four-feet deep soaking pools that are kept at about 108 degrees F, co-ed hot baths, a geothermal steam room, and of course the large outdoor pool for children and adults. There are massage therapies and herbal wraps available to heal or relax you inside and out. The large outdoor pool is similar to a municipal pool in its popularity during summer, when the water is kept at a refreshing 88 degrees. In the heat of summer, it is impossible not to smile right along with the crowd of jubilant youngsters enjoying the fun.

The segregated bathhouses are for adults only and are clean and well kept, but show the age that results from a legacy of long service to the community. At the least, you should be comfortable using the same showers and changing rooms that have served well since the 1950s. The private spa to the rear of the main pool is a recent addition; children are not permitted. The motel facility has 18 rooms, including 4 family units that each can handle six guests. The recreational-vehicle hookups have 8 spaces and can handle class-A motor homes.

Legend has it that the struggle to control the springs had a notable milestone, prior to the white settlers and their government simply wresting away control. In 1866 the regional Ute and Navajo tribes tired of their continual bickering over dominion of the Great Pagosa Springs, and it was decided that a single man would represent each tribe in a winner-take-all fight to the death. The Navajo selected a brawny brave, and the Utes chose U.S. Cavalry Colonel Albert Pfieffer, their (perhaps expendable) ally and enemy of the Navajo. A small but clever man who once scouted under Kit Carson, Pfieffer chose the weapon of the contest to be Bowie knives, and used his deft quickness and compact size to end the battle rather hastily, to the Ute advantage. Ultimately, due to the continual influx of settlers, treaties between the U.S. government and the Utes simply collapsed with repeated abuses of the trust, and the Indians were exiled. This was not a pretty time in the history of what was then still a young nation.

As much a community, public facility as a historic site, the Spa Motel has something for just about everyone, with its various pools and baths. It offers convenient access to town, it is situated in a vacation wonderland, and it has a rich history; the motel is a nice place to drop anchor and stay awhile.

Area highlights: So much of Colorado is loaded with things to do, especially outdoors. The Pagosa Springs area is true to form, offering an array of activities for visitors. Consider winter sports like snowmobiling, cross-country skiing, snowshoeing, skating, alpine skiing, and snowboarding. Just north of Durango is Purgatory Ski Area, with a summit just less than 11,000 feet in elevation, or Wolf Creek just outside of Pagosa Springs at just less than 12,000 feet and boasting an annual snowfall of 465 inches (nearly 40 feet!). Maybe winter camping is something you always wanted to do. Would you like to mush a team of sled dogs or take a horse-drawn sleigh ride? In summer there is nearly option paralysis, with so many things to do and places to go. For a really special excursion, board the Cumbres and Toltec Scenic Railroad in either Chama, New Mexico or Antonito, Colorado and ride through 64 miles of spectacular scenery. The Durango-Silverton Railroad is similar in its traverse of superb scenery. West of Durango is the Ute Mountain Tribal Park and the Mesa Verde National Park where you can see ancient cliff dwellings and Anasazi ruins, or view them in the nearby Chimney Rock Archaeological Area. Colorado's largest wilderness area, the Weminuche Wilderness, offers exceptional hiking, hunting, camping, rafting, horse trails, wildlife viewing, and photography. Navajo Lake is just 30 minutes south of Pagosa Springs, and it provides water skiing, sailing, wind surfing, and fishing. Echo Lake State Park is just outside town, and the lake is stocked with fish. The San Juan River courses through Pagosa Springs, just a couple of blocks from the spa, and it plays host to kayakers, rafters, and anglers. There is an annual Folk Festival over the Labor Day weekend. A 27-hole championship golf course and tennis complex near town will keep your swing tuned.

Stop by the Chamber of Commerce across the street for self-guided tour maps for car travel, mountain biking, or walking. A cultural, historic, and outdoor paradise, Pagosa Springs is a continual adventure.

SW 10

Splashland Pool

General description: Community swimming pool.
Location: Just north of Alamosa in south central Colorado.
Development: Large public pool and children's swimming area.
Best time to visit: Memorial Day to Labor Day.
Restrictions: None.
Access: Easy and convenient year-round access on public roads.
Water temperature: Moderate and variable, from 85 to 95 degrees F.
Services: Full services available in Alamosa.
Camping: None.
Maps: Alamosa East Quadrangle; Rio Grande National Forest.
GPS coordinates: N 37 29 19 W 105 51 31
Finding the springs: From Alamosa in south-central Colorado, drive north 1.4 miles on State Highway 17. Splashland's pink and brown brick is easily visible from the road.

Overview: If you ask any normal kid between the ages of 5 and 15 about his or her favorite things to do on a warm summer afternoon, undoubtedly swimming will be near the top of the list. Water just seems to draw small people like a magnet, and the Splashland Pool is exactly the kind of place you would want them to enjoy. In Colorado there are a handful of community-centric pools that are clean, fun places to spend a summer afternoon, and this is one of them. If it seems on a hot July afternoon that the lifeguards know most of the kids' names in this 150-feet-long pool, it's probably because they do. For the communities that surround Alamosa, Splashland is a wholesome meeting place for their children and buckets of fun for everyone. It has been a familiar place for over 40 years.

The main pool is large, and deep enough at the diving-board end (10 feet), but it seems to have been set up with the younger set in mind because half of the pool is shallow enough for beginners to swim and frolic safely in the 95-degree F water. Corrugated translucent fiberglass walls painted disarmingly pink surround the pool, and there is even a sun deck on the bathhouse roof. The snack bar offers its goods at surprisingly inexpensive prices, but this seems in keeping with the flavor of a place whose mission is for the community good.

The two artesian wells that feed Splashland are only 40 feet apart, just west of the pool. They are 2,600 feet deep. In winter, when the pool is closed, they are used for domestic hot water and space heating of the ranch buildings. The original pool was built on the family ranch in 1955 by Lloyd Jones, and

Splashland Pool, Colorado Alligator Farm, Sand Dune Pool, Mineral Hot Springs, Valley View Hot Springs

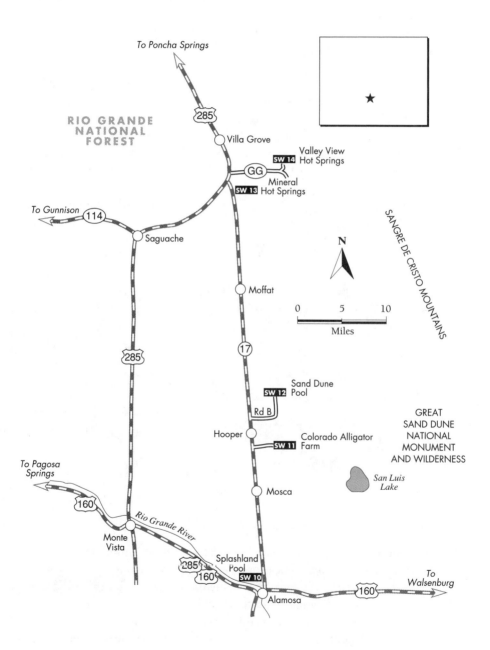

operated as a family business for 30 years.

In the agricultural surrounds of Alamosa, the network of irrigation ditches were responsible for the deaths of children who naturally enough were drawn to the water, but it was not until the pool was built that a viable safer alternative was available.

In the 1980s the pool was offered to the City of Alamosa, but because of liability issues, expense, and potential maintenance problems, the offer was refused. A handful of motivated and dedicated locals, including current manager Judy Crisco, launched a campaign whose motto was SOS (Save Our Splashland), with the intention of securing private funding to keep the pool operating in the community. The story reads like a fairy tale of hard work and heroic efforts on their part, and the large heart of Jones, ultimately leading to the formation of Splashland Hot Springs Inc. In 1987 the new group took over ownership, and ten years later the facility was fully paid for. They are celebrating that fact by adding a small water slide. What a perfect addition to the pool that survived through inspiration and generous hearts for the benefit of the community's children.

On a given summer afternoon in August you might find seven or eight lifeguards keeping watchful eyes over 200 joyful, splashing faces. In the morning the pool is used for lap swimmers and lessons until 10 A.M., after which the complexion changes and the kids rule. By about 4 P.M. the crowds have evaporated and the mood changes again to peace and quiet. With a maximum outlay of $4 per day, Alamosa could scarcely hope for a better place for generations to splash together. It is truly "For the Kids."

Area highlights: Among the numerous recreational opportunities in this area, count several other hot-springs developments. The Colorado Alligator Farm is close, as is the Great Sand Dunes National Monument, Zapata Falls, and the Alamosa-Monte Vista National Wildlife Refuge. The Sangre De Cristo Mountains are loaded with outdoor recreation, from hunting and fishing to rock climbing, camping, and hiking. San Luis Lakes State Park is nearby, and so are museums and old mining ghost towns if you enjoy the area's cultural heritage. If you just want to relax, there are numerous golf courses to master, or perhaps you would like to take a trip on the Cumbres and Toltec Scenic Railroad, which tracks south through the San Juan Mountains. So much to do, and so little time.

SW 11

Colorado Alligator Farm

(See map on page 93)

General description: An aquaculture farm growing alligators and fish with an assortment of reptiles and native wildlife on-site. This is not a swimming site for people.

Location: South-central Colorado, a few miles north of Alamosa.

Development: Aquaculture, exotic wildlife, and greenhouses with visitor center.

Best times to visit: Summer may be best, but the access is good any time of year and wildlife congregates at the warm-water site all year long.

Restrictions: No public swimming; fee area.

Access: Easy and convenient year-round access by public roads.

Water temperature: Alligator pools are kept at about 87 degrees F.

Services: None available on-site. Nearest full services are in Hooper or Alamosa.

Camping: None.

Map: Hooper East Quadrangle.

GPS coordinates: N 37 42 22 W 105 52 20.

Finding the springs: Easily accessible from most directions in the south-central part of Colorado, the simplest approach is to drive north of Alamosa on State Highway 17 for 17 miles and watch for the sign for the alligator farm on the east side of the highway (if you reach Hooper, you've gone too far). Traveling south about 30 miles from the junction of State Highway 285 and SH 17, you will go through Moffat. Continuing on for about 2.7 miles south of Hooper, you will see the sign. The 'gator farm entrance is a quarter-mile east of SH 17 on a dirt road.

Overview: There are some beautiful hot springs around the great State of Colorado, with a diverse array of secluded and public locations that attract an equally diverse set of swimmers and soakers. Many of the warm-water sites are clothing-optional by custom, and some simply require that you wear acceptable bathing attire. There is one thermal pool, however, that you may want to think very carefully about jumping into, not because it is too hot or because the swimmers have no swimsuits, but because the ripples in the water are made by alligators 8 feet long! Unique to the state, this is a successful aquaculture business that uses the warm water from a geothermal well 2,000 feet deep to grow Rocky Mountain white tilapia, a fish raised for food. With a refreshingly efficient ecosystem perspective, American alligators are grown on premises to make good use of the byproducts of the small fish-processing plant, and bask comfortably (it would seem) in the thermal influx that warms their ponds.

Owners Erwin and Lynne Young have a commercial farming operation that makes innovative use of water heated by the earth. These high desert hot pools (they are at an elevation of 7,500 feet) beckon to numerous animals besides those fascinatingly fearsome reptiles that seem oddly at home so far from their native habitat in places like the Florida Everglades. Surveying the grounds of the Colorado Alligator Farm, you will see an assortment of buildings, the Tropical Ecozone among them. This is the main fish production and hydroponics area, flush with tropical plants that enjoy the warm environs. Another building houses an assortment of reptiles ranging from boa constrictors to turtles and a few bazillion tilapia fry. There is even a small gift shop where you can purchase alligator meat or souvenir hats and postcards. Nearby is a five-acre reservoir and wildlife zone that you may see close up and personal by renting a small boat. The warm-water effluent from the fish and alligator farming operations is used to feed a small lake, which is also habitat for an assortment of ducks, geese, herons, and other native wildlife. In the lake, for a fee of $10 for the day you may try your fishing skills and keep up to five fish from the assortment of stocked specimens. Largemouth bass are catch and release only, but if you land a carp you may feed that to the 'gators! The Colorado Alligator Farm did not begin life as a tourist establishment, but over time it has grown in notoriety and size as a result of taking in unwanted reptiles that include four spectacled caimans, Burmese and ball pythons, box turtles, and of course, alligators. A staff herpetologist attends to the many reptiles that have come to call this home, and stood guard as the first "native" Colorado alligator was born here in September 1997. There are almost a hundred alligators in residence now.

In an area of Colorado with numerous natural hot springs and developed geothermal wells, this site is a unique and interesting change of pace. Aside from being in a recreational utopia, the south-central part of the state is full of interesting history and people. You may find a visit to the Colorado Alligator Farm a fun way to enjoy hot water with others who have a much longer history of doing so than humans do.

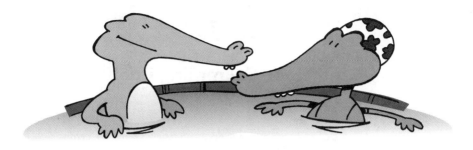

Area highlights: There is much to see and do in Colorado's San Luis Valley, including enjoying numerous other hot springs (for humans). The Sangre De Cristo Mountains are a beautiful centerpiece for recreational opportunity that includes sightseeing, hiking, fishing, and hunting in a place known for its abundant wildlife. Nearby is Great Sand Dunes National Monument and Wilderness, the Blanca Wetlands, the Alamosa-Monte Vista National Wildlife Refuge, and Zapata Falls. Golf courses seem to be everywhere, or you can take a day and ride on the Cumbres and Toltec Scenic Railroad, which boards south of Alamosa at Antonito and crosses over into New Mexico 11 times as it tours the beautiful San Juan Mountains to the south. San Luis Lakes State Park is an easy drive from here, or you can visit Fort Garland, where famous trapper and explorer Kit Carson once was commander. Southern Colorado is resplendent in its vibrant history, which seems not to have faded much over the years. Mexican and Native American cultures flavor the chronicles of the San Luis area, as much as old mining ghost towns and cattle ranches.

SW 12

Sand Dune Swimming Pool

(See map on page 93)

General description: Large outdoor pool and family swimming center.
Location: Twenty miles north of Alamosa in south-central Colorado.
Development: Swimming pool, decks, greenhouse lounge, and family picnic area.
Best times to visit: Spring, summer, and fall take advantage of picnic facilities.
Restrictions: None.
Access: Easy and convenient year-round access by public roads.
Water temperature: Moderate and variable, from 98 to 102 degrees F.
Services: Some services in Hooper, but nearest full services are south in Alamosa.
Camping: None.
Maps: Deadman Camp Quadrangle; San Isabel National Forest; Rio Grande National Forest.
GPS coordinates: N 37 46 42 W 105 51 20.
Finding the springs: From Alamosa, drive north on State Highway 17 about 20 miles to the little town of Hooper; continue on SH 17 for 1 mile beyond Hooper and look for a sign for Road B on the right (the east side of the road). From the Road B turnoff, head east on a well-maintained gravel road for 1.5 miles, and turn left at the T in the road onto Road 63, traveling north again for about 1 mile. On your left, the pool is impossible to miss since there is little besides sagebrush flats to distract you. You can drive your motor home right up to the pool.

Overview: The "Hooper Pool," as it is affectionately called by locals, technically is not quite a hot springs, since it is fed by warm water from a 4,400-feet-deep well that delivers water instead of black, gooey oil. Drilled in the early 1930s as an exploratory oil well, the same fault that spawns the other hot springs and warm-water sources in the area was struck. The consolation prize is 118-degree F water that in the long run is perhaps a more valuable commodity than the oil that was sought by the early drillers. The legacy of wildcat drilling in southern Colorado has long since lost its luster, and what lives on is a very nicely developed contribution to the community, the Sand Dunes Swimming Pool.

The San Luis Valley is home to a remarkable diversity of recreational opportunity, and this pool is typical of the small, serendipitous gems awaiting the

There's great community fun at Sand Dune Pool. PHOTO BY SHARI HARMON

vacationer, as well as the regular visitor. Over its varied 65-year history it has endured stardom and collapse not unlike other geothermal sites in the American West. Initially built as a swimming facility to take advantage of the wonderfully sulfur-free hot water, it has suffered through extended periods of disuse. During the early 1980s an aquaculture operation on this site raised catfish for human consumption. Another period of dormancy ended in the summer of 1995 when the pool was deepened to a maximum depth of 10 feet, uncovering three layers of pool floor, just as if it were a buried city upon another city, like the archaeological digs dating back to ancient Europe and Africa. Though Sharie and Ed Harmon's new facility is comfortably modern, it is impossible not to wonder about the early swimmers who enjoyed the site's hot water. Were they just regular townsfolk of the area or tourists passing through on their way to other places? What was their world like when the pre-catfish pool had only a mud-covered, wood-board bottom and there were no microwave ovens warming patrons' poolside hot dogs or people casually chatting on their cellular phones from the sun deck? The mountains and sand dunes were the same, but not much else was.

At the west end of this large pool is a greenhouse-like covered area that makes watching your youngsters in the separate kiddy pool a pleasure. There you may escape the wind or noise outside, but still be part of the main pool zone visually. Think of it as a large greenhouse lounge. Out by the main pool is a snack bar with a wide assortment of munchies—like pizza and burritos and thirst-quenching fluids. When was the last time you bought a hot dog for 50 cents? You can even rent or buy pool toys. The changing area is clean and spacious, as is generally the entire "Hooper Pool" complex. Fresh produce and herbs grown hydroponically in the nearby geothermally heated greenhouse are for sale at the front office, too. There is a pleasant creekside grassy area with a volleyball net, hammocks, horseshoe pits, and tables and grills to make an afternoon picnic quite pleasant. The handicap-accessible Sand Dune Pool is open February through November from 10 A.M. to 10 P.M. daily except holidays and on Thursdays, when the pool is drained for cleaning. Rates are affordable; the daily fee is $5, and the discounted senior rate is $2.50. If you seek a friendly, affordable family establishment, this distinctly rural setting with a sweet view of the Sangre De Cristo Mountains is like being invited to a family party at the home of your Uncle Harmon, who just happens to have a great swimming pool in his front yard. It's that comfortable and just as much fun.

Area highlights: As close as this pool is to the Sangre De Cristo (Spanish for "Blood of Christ") mountains, you will have numerous recreational opportunities. The Rio Grande National Forest to the west and the San Isabel National Forest to the east offers virtually limitless outdoor possibilities. There are wildlife sanctuaries, ancient historical sites, and turn-of-the-century ghost towns, as well as more common pursuits like golfing, swimming, river floating, or rock climbing. The Great Sand Dunes National Monument is within view; this wilderness area offers superb hiking and sightseeing. Are you interested in spending a day aboard a reconstructed sightseeing railroad, touring some of southern Colorado's most beautiful mountains (the San Juans) along the New Mexico border? There is much old western history displayed in area museums, in the buildings, and in the graveyards. The Colorado Alligator Farm and Zapata Falls are but a short distance away. No matter what your pleasure, the cultural flavor and outdoor options assure you will have more to do than you will have time for.

SW 13

Mineral Hot Springs

(See map on page 93)

General description: Community-based spa with pools, sun decks, and sauna.
Location: South-central Colorado, 50 miles north of Alamosa.
Development: Pools, decks, sauna, and bathhouse facilities.
Best times to visit: Spring, autumn, and winter are pleasant times to visit.
Restrictions: None.
Access: Easy and convenient year-round access by public roads.
Water temperature: Moderate and variable, from 102 to 108 degrees F.
Services: None. Closest full services are 32 miles north in Salida.
Camping: None.
Maps: Villa Grove Quadrangle; San Isabel National Forest.
GPS coordinates: N 38 10 08 W 10 55 10.
Finding the springs: Located on Colorado State Highway 17 about 32 miles south of Salida and 50 miles north of Alamosa (1 mile south of the junction of State Highway 285 and SH 17), Mineral Hot Springs is easily visible from the road.

Overview: Like many of the hot springs in the West, this unusually hot travertine springs has a history that goes back far before written accounts, and certainly long before the white European settlers began to use the water around 1892. The Ute Indian artifacts were perhaps historically insignificant to the new settlements until about 40 years ago, when Mineral Hot Springs was scoured of its sacred, historical cache. What remains is what brought earlier generations of humans and assorted native wildlife—some of Colorado's clearest, hottest water in the shadows of the stunningly beautiful, 14,000-feet-high Sangre De Cristo Mountains.

In the peaceful, high (7,700 feet in elevation) San Luis Valley of south-central Colorado, you would have found a rowdy dance hall in about 1910. Those were lively times in the early expansion of the American West, and our vision of a dance hall and adjacent hot springs is doubtless much more refined than the rough-and-tumble spirit that sought the community of hot water, dancing, and perhaps a drink or two. By most standards the San Luis Valley is still rather isolated, and thoughts of the hearty folks who clung to their dreams here at the turn of the century may bring admiration and respect to your mind. The area residents worked hard and played hard, so when it came time to go into town after long days or weeks of physically harsh work in demanding country, you might imagine that there were moments of excess in the context of a dance hall and hot springs. Perhaps things were simpler then.

Much later, a hog farm tapped the warm flow before that enterprise, too, failed, leaving only a faded footnote in history to mark its passing. For years the place was host to an "alternative lifestyle" community, a common thread running through the colorful history of so many hot springs. Long held as a private, family-owned development, it has just recently been rebuilt into a delightful spa with exceptional views of the mountains and an uncanny remoteness that belies its easy access.

Five years into a project to renovate the grounds and build a new, clean development, Mineral Hot Springs Spa has been open for two years as a community-oriented, public recreational facility. The husband and wife team of Lotus McElfish and Victor Summers is not new to the world of hot springs and rebuilding a neglected facility, having done so in California years ago. They have done much to upgrade the spa, creating a clean, well-appointed business with three pools, nicely tiled, and surrounded by wooden decks. There are glass windscreens to make soaking more pleasant on windy days, and there are those wonderfully ever-present, open views of the mountains to the east. There is a sauna with aspen-paneled walls and a tidy bathhouse whose floor and showers are heated by the remarkably clear, odorless springs water. Tower Pool is neck

Mineral Hot Springs—relaxing and scenic splendor. PHOTO BY VICTOR SUMMERS

deep, and kept company by two waist-deep pools whose temperatures vary with the seasons. You may pamper yourself with a relaxing full-body massage, or possibly an aloe-calendula facial that is part of an herbal body wrap. There is a small spa shop where you can buy refreshments and look over a collection of local art in the gallery. Swimsuits are required, but if you forgot yours you can borrow one of those kept on hand for just that purpose! This is a daytime facility, open from 10 A.M. to 10 P.M. Thursday through Sunday, with all-day rates just under $10 for visitors and reduced rates for local residents. There is a separate pool area available for private parties, if you prearrange that. All in all, this is a very comfortable, easy place to spend your day.

Area highlights: The Sangre De Cristo (Spanish for "Blood of Christ") Mountains dominate the area, not only with their presence but in the recreational opportunities they provide. In the nearby San Isabel and Rio Grande national forests there is sightseeing, hiking, fishing, and hunting in a place known for its abundant wildlife. Not far away are the Great Sand Dunes National Monument and Wilderness, old mining ghost towns, the Alamosa-Monte Vista National Wildlife Refuge—full of exotic bird life including the rare whooping crane—and Colorado's oldest town, San Luis. Our Lady of Guadalupe is the oldest church in Colorado. Golf courses abound, or you can take a day ride on the Cumbres and Toltec Scenic Railroad that boards south of Alamosa at Antonito and crosses over into New Mexico 11 times as it tours the beautiful San Juan Mountains. You can do some extreme rock climbing in Penitente Canyon or see Fort Garland, where famous trapper and explorer Kit Carson was once commander. The area around Mineral Hot Springs is a vacation paradise, oozing with western history and flavor.

SW 14

Valley View Hot Springs

(See map on page 93)

General description: Secluded naturist development with pools in wooded area.

Location: South-central Colorado, 7 miles from the junction of State Highway 17 and U.S. Highway 285.

Development: Pools, sauna, and overnight accommodations in a natural setting.

Best times to visit: Spring through fall are the prettiest here.

Restrictions: Open only to members (and guests) on weekends; open to the public on weekdays. It is a good idea to call ahead. Closed most of December.

Access: Easy and convenient year-round access on public roads.

Water temperature: Moderate and variable, from 80 to 101 degrees F.

Services: Full services in Villa Grove (12 miles away). Rustic private cabins available, some with kitchen facilities. Advance reservations are recommended.

Camping: Limited recreational-vehicle parking—no hookups. Designated camping areas.

Maps: Valley View Hot Springs Quadrangle; San Isabel National Forest.

GPS coordinates: N 38 11 31 W 105 48 48.

Finding the springs: From Alamosa, drive 50 miles north on SH 17 to the junction of Highway 17 and US 285 and look for County Road GG. Take gravel CR GG to the east for about 7 miles through sagebrush flats and look for a sign on your left. From Poncha Springs on US 285, drive south about 26 miles and at the junction of US 285 and SH 17, take CR GG east for 7 miles.

Overview: Before you leave Valley View Hot Springs, you will believe it is a special place. Though not a style for everyone, it is perhaps in one of the prettiest Colorado settings and blessed with enormous personality. Valley View makes no concessions to pleasing the multitudes, and pity you if you don't care for the place, but there is a waiting list years long to become a member. Enjoying a wonderful view of the isolated, scenic San Luis Valley, crouched on the western doorstep of the exquisite Sangre De Cristo Mountains, you are transported back in time to when things were less crowded, less complex, and less rushed. That alone should commend this hot springs, if your taste runs in the retreat, clothing-optional direction.

Valley View Hot Springs—an idyllic retreat.

Stories of numerous archaeological finds, such as pottery shards and arrowheads, speak to the history of the native Ute Indians—long before the early 1800s when Spanish land grants parceled out the territory as political payoffs and incentives. Though the Native Americans knew and cared nothing of this European version of Manifest Destiny, they came to know its effects when the U.S. Cavalry forced the tribe off the land in the late 1800s. A bitterly sad time in history, reflecting greed and arrogance on the part of the invading settlers, this act nonetheless paved the way for entrepreneur John Everson to develop the site with buildings catering to the mining community. There was a lapse in the ownership and care of Valley View, but the typical "free spirit" community takeover was inevitable.

Some called them hippies, but society has a long-established legacy of those who follow their own set of rules that run contrary to the common view. Neil Seitz came into the picture as an employee but by 1979 was the owner; Neil and his wife, Terry, still own this idyllic hideout. Transformed from a roughshod clubhouse for drifters, hooligans, and peaceniks, it is now a carefully maintained and closely controlled refuge with naturist leanings.

Exclusivity has its rewards, and although Valley View is open to the public, it is still tightly knit in terms of its membership. Open to the public from Sunday evening until Friday afternoon, the limited membership has the place to themselves during the weekend. Members may invite guests on weekends or holidays. Entry and exit is also monitored, as the entrance is a gateway check-in to the resort. If you slip past the front desk, don't be surprised if there is someone waiting for you with a walkie-talkie in hand. The current method of gaining membership status is through an annual lottery, limiting the card-carrying few to a mere 700. Your name would be placed in a hopper in November, with a one in six chance of being drawn. In subsequent years you will have accrued a "preference point" that effectively increases your chances of being selected. It's a simple and fair system very much like state wildlife agencies use to draw lottery winners for limited big-game hunting tags. It is one of the ways Valley View maintains a quality experience for its visitors. This is not a noisy playground for children running around out of control (although there are numerous families with children, especially in summer), nor is disorderly conduct by a band of drunken rowdies allowed. In fact, there is a "quiet hours" policy from 10 P.M. to 8 A.M. that prohibits noisy generators from parked recreational vehicles and similar irritations.

The main pool has concrete decks and is fed by clear, low-sulfur water kept at about 85 degrees F. The water has actually been tested as potable, although consuming it is not recommended. There is an adjacent kiddy pool that is heated to maintain a child-pleasing 102 degrees, using a clever hydroelectric system. Sprinkled through the woods on a series of footpaths are four additional small soaking ponds that are all surrounded by trees and own superb mountain vistas. The ponds vary in size, but comfortably might accommodate four people in their natural settings. There is even a small wood-fueled sauna with its own tiny private pool. When you check into the front office for a visit, there is a hand-painted, picture-window-size map that details the paths, pools, and buildings. The rental cabins and communal facilities (bathrooms, picnic areas, and parking) are just as plump with character as the rest of Valley View Hot Springs, and date back to the early 1900s. They have been updated, many with kitchens, and of course they all have names. Oakhouse has a Windsor upright grand piano in its common room, while the more modern Sunset House is an option if you prefer that. A secluded haven at 8,700 feet in elevation, with views to die for and almost guaranteed to relieve your stress, Valley View is unique in many wonderful ways. It would certainly make the short list of hot springs done well.

Area highlights: The San Luis Valley is ripe with history, some good and some ugly. Still, like most history, it goes back before what anyone can remember, and its clues and lessons are still there for all. The Spanish explorers gave the places names that linger and point to a different time. The "Blood of Christ" (Sangre De Cristo) Mountains are full of scenic beauty and recreational opportunity, as are the San Isabel and Rio Grande (Big River) national forests. There are countless small lakes to photograph, fish in, and camp near, in the vicinity of the 13,000-feet-high Sangre De Cristo peaks. You can float or angle in the Arkansas River, if you enjoy getting wet. Close by is the Great Sand Dunes National Monument and Wilderness, the Alamosa-Monte Vista National Wildlife refuge, San Luis Lakes National Wildlife Area and rock climbing destination Penitente Canyon. There are no fewer than nine "Fourteeners" to climb, just a short jaunt to the south end of the mountain range. The Cumbres and Toltec Scenic Railroad will take you on a narrow-gauge tour of the spectacular San Juan Mountains bordering New Mexico. The town of San Luis is the oldest in Colorado, and Our Lady of Guadalupe is the oldest church in Colorado. Ancient mining ghost towns, museums, and summer festivals all bring the history close. Crestone and Bonanza are two of the ghost towns, although atypical with their quiet histories during relatively lawless times. Home to about 5,000 during its heyday, mine production trailed off around 1915 and today Bonanza has fewer than 25 permanent residents. No matter where you go, there will be adventure and discovery.

SW 15

Salida Hot Springs

General description: Large, community-centered pool and soaking facility.
Location: South-central Colorado on U.S. Highway 50, west of Pueblo.
Development: Nicely developed public swimming and private soaking tubs.
Best time to visit: Since it is an indoor pool, any time of year is comfortable.
Restrictions: None.
Access: Easy and convenient year-round access by public roads.
Water temperature: Moderate and variable, from 90 to 100 degrees F.
Services: Full services available in Salida.
Camping: None.
Maps: Poncha Pass Quadrangle; San Isabel National Forest; Rio Grande National Forest.
GPS coordinates: N 38 30 01 W 105 58 30.
Finding the springs: Salida Hot Springs is centrally located about an hour-and-a-half drive from Alamosa, Pueblo, Gunnison. or Aspen. Take US 50 west of Pueblo to the west end of Salida at Centennial Park. From Interstate 70, just west of Vail, take U.S. Highway 24 south past Buena Vista to U.S. Highway 285; take US 285 to Poncha Springs. At Poncha Springs, go east 5 miles to Salida on US 50. The Salida Hot Springs Pool and Aquatic Center is easily visible from the highway.

Overview: "Salida" is Spanish for *entrance* or *exit*. It is a hospitable community with a beautiful location in the heart of Colorado's mountain country, and it has a swimming pool to make any town proud. Fed by hot water piped from Poncha Springs 5 miles to the west, the community makes great use of the pool complex as a recreational and educational facility. There are three pools in the large indoor center, with the largest featuring a 75-feet-long section with lap lanes and a temperature of about 90 degrees F. A divider at one end functionally separates a 4-feet-deep section that runs the full width of the pool and has a much warmer temperature, 100 degrees, for therapeutic needs and more comfortable soaking. There is also a children's wading pool, only 18 inches deep, that is warmed to about 95 degrees.

In addition to the swimming pools, there are six soaking tubs that can be rented by the hour. Each has a small window and enough seclusion to provide complete relaxation. There is a legend about a man who died in pool number four, but whose energy is said to have remained for those who are sensitive to such things.

Salida Hot Springs, Mount Princeton Hot Springs, Cottonwood Hot Springs

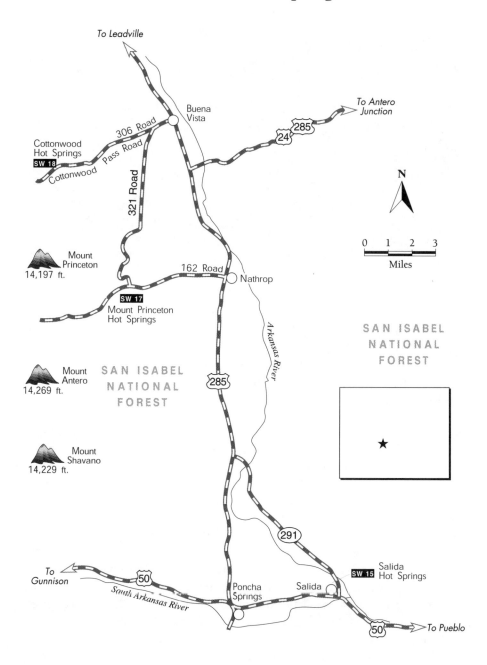

Salida Hot Springs is a big city pool in a small town.

The pool is proudly used by the town of Salida for any number of community activities ranging from the Salida Cyclone Swim Team practice to kayaking lessons to Red Cross swimming certifications. There are always at least two lap lanes reserved for exercise swimmers or training. Almost any time of the year, you will find the pool well attended by locals and visitors who appreciate the clean, tidy facility.

As with most of Colorado's hot springs, the hot water from Poncha Springs was once used by the Ute Indians. Poncha Springs is an assortment of nearly 50 effusions that bubble warm water out on the hillside and along Poncha Creek before the stream joins the Arkansas River. With the settlement of the area by European immigrant miners and railroad workers, Poncha Springs had become an attraction by the late 1860s. With the building of the Denver and Rio Grande Railroad (itself an interesting history of political maneuvering, legal wars, and expensive lobbying) in the Arkansas River Valley, the town of Salida grew by leaps and bounds. Named by former Colorado territorial governor A. C. Hunt and his wife, Salida nearly became the state capitol, and the lavish Jackson Hotel was a prosperous business, depending on the hot water's allure. Poncha Springs was linked formally with Salida by pipeline under a Works Progress Administration project in 1937, creating what became Colorado's largest indoor hot-springs pool. Poncha's main springs are owned by the City of Salida, but the site of most of the effluent is used by the Boy Scouts as a summer base camp. In

June 1938, the main pool was filled with hot water from Poncha Springs, and it has lived up to the predictions of the prosperous union.

Surviving the rugged times of the early West, the springs is now a center-piece for Salida and the surrounding area.

Area highlights: Salida is a scenic area full of recreational opportunity, much of which centers around the San Isabel National Forest and the beautiful high mountains. Blessed with several peaks whose elevations exceed 14,000 feet, called "Fourteeners" (Mount Shavano, Mount Ouray, and Mount Antero are named after Ute Indians), the mountains around Salida serve those who enjoy hiking, wildlife watching, photography, exploring, climbing, four-wheel-drive trekking, fishing, hunting, and dozens of other outdoor exploits. The Arkansas River is known for whitewater rafting, kayaking, and float fishing. Alpine and cross-country skiing is within easy reach, and the area is popular with snowmobilers because of the high-country winter snows.

SW 16

Waunita Hot Springs

General description: Private, family-style guest ranch with large hot-springs pool.

Location: West-central Colorado, about 19 miles east of Gunnison.

Development: The pool is a sideline to the fully outfitted dude ranch.

Best time to visit: Any time of year the pool is great, but summer is best.

Restrictions: The pool is open to guest ranch patrons only.

Access: Reasonably good access most of the year on public roads. Winter and muddy spring seasons may pose some minor access problems.

Water temperature: Moderate and variable, from 95 to 108 degrees F.

Services: Full services are available in Gunnison, 19 miles to the west.

Camping: None.

Maps: Pitkin Quadrangle; Gunnison National Forest; San Isabel National Forest.

GPS coordinates: N 38 30 57 W 106 30 56.

Finding the springs: From Gunnison in west-central Colorado, drive east on U.S. Highway 50 to County Road 887 and turn north onto the gravel road; continue on CR 887 for 8 miles. Waunita Hot Springs Ranch will be on your left, with a sign over the driveway entrance. Look for the unique "horse parking" barn.

Waunita Hot Springs

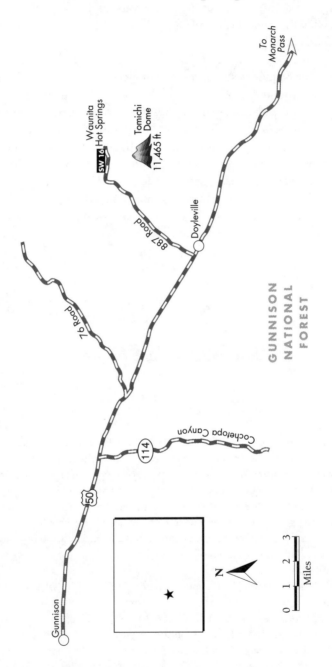

Overview: Along the dirt road from the highway turnoff you will notice a large mound-shaped mountain to the east. That's Tomichi Dome, which at 11,465 feet in elevation is a significant cinder-cone. Technically a *lacolith*—which has to do with underground volcanic magma chambers intruding into surface areas and incidentally bumping into the water table—it is the birthplace of 300,000-gallons-per-day Waunita Hot Springs. On the less scientific side, it is also quite possible that the mournful tears of sorrow from a beautiful Ute Indian maiden created the hot springs. Legend says that long ago she fell deeply in love with a Shoshone warrior who then was killed in battle. So strong was her love, and then her grief upon his death, that she soon died from sheer sadness and was buried in a nearby cave. Where her tears of sorrow fell, the earth weeps eternal springs of hot water.

Some of the hottest springs in the state, they are now part of the Waunita Hot Springs Guest Ranch, and are open only to the guests. They are not the focus of this beautiful little paradise surrounded by the Gunnison National Forest, but merely are an amenity that pampers guests with a large pool, a hot tub, and hot springs-heated buildings and domestic water. The rugged cowboy out front may well be Ryan Pringle, whose wife, Tammy, runs the front desk and whose folks (Rod and Junelle) bought the place in 1962 when they moved up from Texas. Tammy explains that the guest ranch is a busy place where summertime guests stay for 6 days at a time and have a constant menu of Western lifestyle while they are there—hay rides, horse trips, rafting, outdoor cookouts, and the grandeur of the beautiful Sawatch Range mountains in the Gunnison forests just off the Continental Divide. After a long day of outdoor adventure, the big pool out back may be more therapy for happily exhausted muscles than leisurely lounging. There is an acknowledged Christian atmosphere, and the rate schedule sheet will remind you that they do not knowingly accommodate unmarried couples in the same unit. Alcohol is not permitted on the premises. This is a family operation with wholesome, old-fashioned values and practices. It feels good.

Temperance was not always the rule in Waunita's long and varied history. Like many of Colorado's old hot-springs developments, this one saw numerous owners from the native Ute Indians to those with simple wooden bathhouses and some with visions of grandeur including orchestras, extravagant hotels, and the opulence of wealth. The property was patented in 1884 and was long a popular destination for locals from the Gunnison area. The area history includes a sawmill down the road, a log bathhouse and hotel, invading hordes of area miners, hotels that burned to the ground, and a short-lived baseball camp. There was even a doctor from Chicago who owned Waunita, believing her "radium water" was the link between spiritual and physical worlds, not to mention a panacea for ailments of the flesh from rheumatism to cancer. Written chronicles and photographs in Junelle Pringle's history scrapbook reveal the typical rise to

Waunita Hot Springs: the dude pool.

greatness and sad fall to dilapidated abandonment. From quiet local picnic grounds to bawdy days of gambling and drinking to years of renowned status as a health sanitarium, the hot springs have flowed and watched it all go by. In the Pringles' front room you will find the scrapbook that rivals an encyclopedia volume in size, with a chronology of owners and events that far exceed the scope of this book. If you elect to become a registered guest, you will enjoy reading the colorful archive, I am certain.

In the back of the guest ranch is a pool of dimensions that would be the envy of many large hotels. There is a hot tub and segregated bathhouse facilities. The water, besides being maintained at soothing temperatures, is clear and almost entirely free of any sulfurous odors. The water slide and basketball hoop are smile-makers for the children, and it is again clear that the emphasis is on family entertainment in a wholesome, Western way. The list is long for people who want a slice of that pie, and the openings are usually booked well in advance. Though the ranch operates year-round, the schedule is much reduced except in summer months. Beautifully located in a scenic valley, you can enjoy a well-run guest ranch whose hot-springs pool is an accouterment as grand as the scale of your Waunita Hot Springs escape.

Area highlights: Monarch and Crested Butte Mountain are two nearby alpine skiing areas, but Nordic skiing and snowmobiling opportunities are everywhere in winter. The San Isabel and Gunnison national forests are full of outdoor recreation from hiking, biking, and climbing (there are numerous "Fourteeners" nearby) to hunting, fishing, and water sports. Just south of Gunnison is the Curecanti National Recreation Area, where the Gunnison River makes Blue Mesa Reservoir and the scenic Black Canyon of the Gunnison. Rafting, kayaking, and all variety of water sports are offered in the area's waterways. Taylor Park Reservoir is in a beautiful location northeast of Gunnison, and if you like to hike to remote mountain lakes, the high country just east of the Divide has dozens you can seek out. The West Elk Wilderness to the northwest is a perfect area to ride a horse into remote country and see the land unchanged from a thousand years ago. For every season, there are wondrous options to explore.

SW 17

Mount Princeton Hot Springs

(See map on page 109)

General description: Family lodge and restaurant, with multiple pools.
Location: Southwest of Denver between Buena Vista and Salida.
Development: Several hot mineral pools, creekside soaking, and water slide.
Best times to visit: Spring, summer, and fall offer great outdoor recreation.
Restrictions: None.
Access: Easy and convenient year-round access on public roads.
Water temperature: Moderate and variable by season, from 85 to 105 degrees F.
Services: Lodging, restaurant, and bar on-site. Nearest full services are in Buena Vista.
Camping: None.
Maps: Mount Antero Quadrangle; San Isabel National Forest; Gunnison National Forest.
GPS coordinates: N 38 43 58 W 106 09 41.
Finding the springs: From Buena Vista, head south for 6 miles on U.S. Highway 24, past the junction with US 285, staying on US 285 to Nathrop. From Nathrop, turn west on County Road 162 and travel just over 4 miles, where you will see signs for Mount Princeton Hot Springs on your left. From Salida, take State Highway 291 north to the junction with US 285 and continue north to Nathrop. From Nathrop, follow the directions above.

Mount Princeton Hot Springs has a rich history. Photo courtesy Mount Princeton Hot Springs

Overview: Enjoying some of the hottest water in the State of Colorado, the area around Mount Princeton Hot Springs is also some of the most scenic mountain country to be found. Nearby, the Collegiate Peaks and more than a dozen others honor you with impressive elevations between 13,000 feet and 14,000 feet or more. Mount Princeton Hot Springs has been in some sort of boom and bust cycle for over a hundred years, from grand mansions in a mining boomtown to abandoned ghost town. Now the site of a nicely developed family lodge featuring pools and a water slide, it is the clear hot water that remains constant.

Back in the days when this part of the world first saw an infusion of European settlement, there was a scramble to find new, untapped sources of gold and silver. The country had no roads, few places to buy supplies, and sometimes-hostile natives who might justifiably be annoyed that the white people were harvesting from the land as if it were theirs for the taking. Those were boom and bust days for mining towns whose fortunes rose and fell with the amount of gold or silver that came out of the ground. The drainage in which Mount Princeton Hot Springs nestles was witness to a tremendous amount of that sort of history. It is a legacy of mining wealth, railroading, and big dreams that flowered and wilted.

Chalk Creek is the stream flowing past Mount Princeton Hot Springs, and it was the reason for all the excitement in the mid-1800s, because there was gold to be found nearby. Although the history is a bit fuzzy, it is estimated that over $60 million in gold and silver came out of the mines on Chalk Creek before the turn of the last century. To put it into better perspective, that was when you could buy a loaf of bread for about three cents. A million dollars was a *lot* of money, and it is what fueled the development of railroads to service the towns of Romley, St. Elmo, Iron City, and Nathrop. Mount Princeton Hot Springs was there to grow with the boom.

A surveyor named D. H. Heywood was responsible for the original government survey of the area, and took ownership of the springs property as payment for his labors. The stage station, freight depot, and hotel that was built there overlooked what is now the bathhouse where some of the numerous springs bubble from the ground. Later, as the Mary Murphy Mine (the area's prime producer) spawned greater wealth, a consortium of miners and businessmen built a grand three-stories-tall hotel. The foreclosure of railroading into the valley crashed hopes for further development until a millionaire from Kansas City named Gafford anteed up the money to build a fabulous four-story hotel of a truly magnificent proportion and style. Exotic woods from all over the world and over a hundred rooms made up this showpiece. There was custom monogrammed silverware, a freight elevator, and even a crude intercom system. Impressive grounds with stonework and ponds, enclosed hot pools, and a golf course made a splendid display of wealth, but they too were destined to fall into disrepair when the Mary Murphy closed in 1924 and the last railroad pulled out. An extensive assortment of owners and foreclosures followed, and the old hotel woodwork ended up in a housing development in Texas.

Finally, in 1960, new owner Dennis Osborn began building the series of pools and lodge that remain today.

The hot springs produce 175,000 gallons of 130-degree F water over a 24-hour period, feeding a large pool often used for lap swimming by locals. That pool has a partially covered entrance awning from the old bathhouse, which dates back to about 1850. The pool is immediately adjacent to Chalk Creek, and there are hot-water inlets into the creek, attracting bathers who snuggle into pockets of warmth amid the flowing water. Up on the hillside, there are mineral pools and a 300-feet-long water slide, as well as motel-style rooms and a conference center. The hot springs are even used to heat the main lodge building.

This is a very comfortable, complete resort that makes fine use of the natural hot springs, but it may be the stunning views of Mount Antero and Mount Princeton that bring you back, as much as the fine soaking.

Area highlights: The nearby Collegiate Range peaks, a spectacular collection of 14,000-feet-high mountains, were named for the Ivy League schools attended by the survey and cartography crew that first mapped the range. With names like Princeton, Harvard, Columbia, and Yale, the mountains are perhaps still more impressive than their namesake schools, as they offer a wonderful opportunity for recreation from climbing, hiking, photography, and skiing to investigating old ghost towns like St. Elmo and Romley. The nearby Arkansas River is famous for its whitewater rafting, and the San Isabel National Forest is full of places to hunt, fish, or explore in a four-wheel-drive vehicle. The Colorado Division of Wildlife runs the Chalk Cliffs Trout Hatchery just down the road, and makes good use of the water warmed by the thermal springs to reduce the growing time of their fish by half.

Monarch Ski Resort is a short drive away, and there are endless places to snowmobile and cross-country ski in the national forests.

SW 18

Cottonwood Hot Springs

(See map on page 109)

General description: Rustic, fully developed hot springs with overnight accommodations, in a scenic recreation area.

Location: Central Colorado, south of Vail on State Highway 24.

Development: Fully developed site with multiple pools and creekside tubs.

Best time to visit: It is accessible any time of year.

Restrictions: Owner prefers that overnight guests not bring dogs.

Access: Easy and convenient access by public roads.

Water temperature: Moderate and variable by season and pool.

Services: Overnight accommodations. Food is available only by special prearrangement. The nearest full facilities are 6 miles away in Buena Vista.

Camping: No Camping.

Maps: Buena Vista West Quadrangle; San Isabel National Forest; Gunnison National Forest.

GPS coordinates: N 38 48 46 W 106 13 33.

Finding the springs: Drive south out of Denver on Interstate 25 and take U.S. Highway 285 west to Buena Vista, a trip of about 110 miles. From Colorado Springs, take U.S. Highway 24 west for about 90 miles to Buena Vista. From Interstate 70 between Glenwood Springs and Vail, take the exit for US 24 to the south and drive about 60 miles to Buena Vista. Once you are in the small town of Buena Vista, look for County Road 306 at the traffic light and drive south about 5.3 miles. Cottonwood Hot Springs will be just across the creek on your right, with a sign telling you that you have arrived. If you cross Cottonwood Pass (12,126 feet in elevation), you have gone too far!

Overview: Visiting Cottonwood Hot Springs may be a spiritual venture. There is something fundamentally spiritual about any geothermal waters, perhaps simply because they are nature's very own, and as natural and unprocessed as anything can be in this modern world we call home. But, there are some places where internal soothing is afforded as much attention as the warmth enveloping your body while you soak luxuriously in a hot pot. While some places may obtain their hot water from an abandoned oil well that taps an aquifer fault, or possibly pipe their water from an underground source several miles distant, Cottonwood is a gravity-fed mineral spa. There is an assortment of pools both large and small, as well as creekside hot tubs. Cottonwood Hot Springs is very much a work-in-progress operation, the dream and daily toil of Cathy Manning, who has owned the business for ten years and runs it with a pragmatic spiritualism and seemingly endless endurance. Most everyone there seems to move to a cadence slightly slower than that of the rest of humanity, and with an enviable look of contentment.

You might gain some insight into the place as a reflection of its owner when you know that Cottonwood has an e-mail address, yet Cathy professes to be blissfully illiterate in the computer world. It is a wonderful blend of an age-old, gravity-fed warm-water flow into simple river-rock pools and decked fiberglass spas next to Cottonwood Creek. There is a large building that serves as a dormitory, and cabins that have their own private mini-pools; or you can camp in an Indian teepee. This is not a four-star hotel, and to be so would fly in the face of the natural, relaxed environment that so deftly unruffles your mood. There are assorted small animals like rabbits, chipmunks, and birds sauntering about in a way that makes you wonder if you are background in a Disney movie. It is hard to put your finger on just why this place seems so casual and earthy.

Development at Cottonwood dates back to 1876, and prior to that, of course, the Ute Indians made regular use of the springs for centuries as a spiritual retreat site. Though it is difficult to assign indisputable evidence to any curative properties, this and many other mineral water hot springs has a history

Unkink your mind and body at Cottonwood Hot Springs.

of patrons who adhere to that belief. One thing is for sure, by the time you leave you will be more relaxed and "centered" than when you arrived.

The Cottonwood creed holds itself to be "a holistic and spiritual center and . . . haven for healing, growth, rejuvenation and restoration of the body/mind/spirit." I think "healing" is probably the key operative word, since there seems to be an emphasis on letting that which is bruised—whether mind or body—recover in the supportive, relaxed environment. That is not to imply that you will come in using a cane and leave doing cartwheels, but simply that healing is an internal thing, at least in part, that happens when you make the frowns of stress evaporate.

The babble of Cottonwood Creek is never far from your ears, and the cabins perched along its banks avail themselves of the water music continually. Each cabin has a small soaking pool fed by the gravity system of hot-water pipes. Though small, the buildings are very pleasantly decorated in period décor that is about to cycle back into vogue, and they welcome you with the intentional lack of distracting telephones or televisions. The dorm rooms are part of the main building, which looks much as if it were moved from a western movie set after having seen a few gunfights and falling stuntmen. There is a restaurant and dining room combination that once was open regularly but took too much of Cathy's time, so it now is available only for groups by advance booking. There's a common room, much the same as a lodge lobby, complete with eclectic furnishings to match the varied library contents. Regrettably, there is a phone available there and a TV/VCR for those who must wean themselves slowly from technology's grip. Rates vary by season and occupancy, and in season you might be well advised to book ahead to avoid being disappointed.

If you were flying over the area in your Cessna 172, you could look down and see that the trio of main pools are surprisingly similar in outline to the chubby Buddha, and it would occur to you that it was not quite accidental, given the philosophy of Cottonwood. The pools are built of smooth river rock and assembled with countless hours of masons' labor and are accented with colorful flower gardens. The biggest pool is about 20 feet by 45 feet, and has a variable depth of up to about 4 feet. The smaller pools are stair-stepped together and share a changing room close to the creek. Small, nicely decked private spas terrace up the hill close to the creek, all having wooden privacy shields and open views of the rushing brook. Always in sight are the graceful and aged cottonwood trees that adorn the stream banks. The water is strikingly clear and reveals relatively low levels of mineral content, especially sulfur, making this a naturally sweet and unfiltered soaking medium so pure as to be potable. Deep into the canyon on the way to Cottonwood Pass, and in the shadow of the Collegiate Peaks (so named for the early surveyors with Ivy League educations), evening simmers long before giving way to darkness. What a gentle place to listen to the creek's chatter and watch the chickens and rabbits go about their animal chores.

It is more than just the relaxing attitude that settles your outlook here at Cottonwood. You can spoil yourself with a tantalizing variety of unique massage therapies, including traditional Thai, Japanese, and Chinese. They offer "chair massage" based on original Chinese acupressure techniques. The liberation of your spirit shifts with the onset of evening darkness, and the pool rules change from a family standard (bathing suits are required) to a clothing-optional adult atmosphere. The streamside hot tubs are always open to clothing-optional rules. In summer, the pools are open from 8 A.M. to midnight, but in winter they close by 10 P.M. For one more thought about relaxation that may intrigue you, ask Cathy about the Sensory Deprivation Flotation Tank.

Area highlights: This part of Colorado is the mountainous high country that many folks think of when they think of Colorado. Within hiking distance of Cottonwood is Mount Princeton, rising to more than 14,000 feet in elevation. In fact, you have an impressive selection of easily accessible "Fourteeners" from which to choose, if that is your bent.

The Gunnison National Forest is known for producing quality elk and deer hunting, but there also is excellent fishing in lakes and streams, and reservoirs like Antero or Taylor Park. The Arkansas River is regionally known as a superb whitewater rafting destination. If you are intrigued by Western history, just down the road is Saint Elmo, one of Colorado's best-preserved ghost towns. Known as Saturday Night Town to some 2,000 people back in the 1880s, it was the town at the end of the railroad line. Other little ghost towns just a stone's throw away from Saint Elmo are Romley and Hancock. Mountain biking, four-wheeling, and photography are great pursuits in this rugged mountain splendor. In winter, snowmobiling is very popular in the Cottonwood Pass area, and Monarch Ski Area enjoys a local reputation as an undiscovered gem. Of course, cross-country skiing is also a great opportunity, with so much high-elevation backcountry close at hand. Relaxing up to your neck in the rejuvenative waters of Cottonwood Hot Springs, you can take pause to consider the paradise of outdoor recreation awaiting you.

Appendix A

This appendix is a cross-reference list of the hot springs in specialized categories. The table of contents lists the locations by general geography. This appendix categorizes the springs according to different criteria. The lists represent the opinions of the author, and are intended to help the reader select potential sites to visit based on factors other than physical location.

Traditional Family-Oriented Hot Springs

This list includes locations that generally require bathing suits and that have an emphasis on public, family facilities. Simply because a hot springs does not appear on this list does *not* imply that the management there dislikes families with children, only that those named below are in my opinion the most suited for taking a vanload of kids to play for an afternoon. They are listed alphabetically.

>   Eldorado Springs
>   Glenwood Hot Springs
>   Indian Springs
>   Mount Princeton Hot Springs
>   Ouray Hot Springs
>   Salida Hot Springs
>   Sand Dune Pool
>   Spa Motel (Pagosa Springs)
>   Splashland Pool
>   Trimble Hot Springs
>   Twin Peaks Motel

Clothing-Optional Hot Springs

The locations listed here are simply those with clothing-optional or naturist policies. That does not exclude them from family participation, for indeed many of them welcome and encourage families. The springs named below may be exclusively or partially clothing-optional, meaning some have schedules allowing both. They are listed in alphabetical order.

>   Conundrum Hot Springs
>   Cottonwood Hot Springs

Desert Reef Beach Club
Orvis Hot Springs
Rainbow Hot Springs
South Canyon Hot Springs
Strawberry Park Hot Springs
Valley View Hot Springs
Well at Brush Creek

BEST BETS FOR PROFESSIONAL PAMPERING

Most of the developed hot springs offer therapeutic massages, body wraps, and personal pampering services to some degree, but there are some that in my opinion have a special emphasis on these arts. The list below reflects the author's view of the best places to go if that is your priority. They are listed in alphabetical order.

Cottonwood Hot Springs
Hot Sulphur Springs
Indian Springs
Mineral Hot Springs
Orvis Hot Springs
Valley View Hot Springs
Wiesbaden Hot Springs
Yampah Spa and Vapor Caves

GREAT GETAWAYS

For some people, a big part of the reason to go to a hot springs is for the relaxation and "de-stressing" for which they are justly famous. That may mean a remote location or a resort that offers a great soak, a good restaurant, and a nice place to stay. For many, romance is a vital part of the getaway. This alphabetical list will point you to springs with great potential for a relaxing, romantic, and comfortable escape.

Box Canyon Hot Springs
Conundrum Hot Springs
Cottonwood Hot Springs
Desert Reef Beach Club
Hot Sulphur Springs
Mineral Hot Springs
Mount Princeton Hot Springs

Orvis Hot Springs
Rainbow Hot Springs
South Canyon Hot Springs
Spring Inn (Pagosa Springs)
Strawberry Park Hot Springs
Valley View Hot Springs
Waunita Hot Springs
Wiesbaden Hot Springs

APPENDIX B

HOT SPRINGS ADDRESSES

Northwest

NW 1 Steamboat Hot Springs
Steamboat Springs Health and
    Recreation
P.O. Box 1211
136 Lincoln Avenue
Steamboat Springs, CO 80477
(970) 879-1828

NW 2 Strawberry Park Hot Springs
P.O. Box 773332
44200 County Road 36
Steamboat Springs, CO 80477
(970) 879-0342
www.computerwz.com/hot_sprgs.htm

NW 3 Hot Sulphur Springs
P.O. Box 85
Hot Sulphur Springs, CO 80451
(970) 887-2830

NW 4 Indian Springs Resort
P.O. Box 1990
302 Soda Creek Road
Idaho Springs, CO 80452
(303) 989-6666
www.indianspringsresort.com

NW 5 South Canyon Hot Springs
N/A

NW 6 Glenwood Hot Springs
P.O. Box 308
Glenwood Springs, CO 81602
(970) 945-6571; or (800) 537-7946
    (Toll-free within Colorado)
www.hotspringspool.com

NW 7 Yampah Spa and Vapor Caves
709 East Sixth Street
Glenwood Springs, CO 81601
(970) 945-0667

NW 8 Conundrum Hot Springs
N/A

Northeast

NE 1 Eldorado Springs
294 Artesian Drive
Eldorado Springs, CO 80015
(303) 499-1316

Southeast

SE 1 The Well at Brush Creek
0001 Malibu Boulevard
U.S. Highway 50 West
Penrose, CO 81240
(719) 372-9250; or (800) 898-WELL

SE 2 The Desert Reef Beach Club
P.O. Box 503
1194 County Road 110
Florence, CO 81240
(719) 784-6134

Southwest

SW 1 Orvis Hot Springs
1585 County Road 3
Ridgeway, CO 81432
(970) 626-5324

SW 2 Twin Peaks Motel
P.O. Box 320
125 Third Avenue
Ouray, CO 81427-0320
(970) 325-4427; FAX: (970) 325-4477

SW 3 Ouray Hot Springs
P.O. Box 468
1000 Main Street
Ouray, CO 81427
(970) 325-4638

SW 4 Box Canyon Lodge and Hot Springs
P.O. Box 439
45 Third Avenue
Ouray, CO 81427
(970) 325-4981; or (800) 327-5080
ouraycolorado.com/boxcanyn.html
bcm@rmii.com

SW 5 Wiesbaden Hot Springs
P. O. Box 349
625 Fifth Avenue
Ouray, CO 81427
(970) 325-4347; FAX: (970) 325-4358
wiesbaden@gwe.net

SW 6 Trimble Hot Springs
6475 County Road 203
Durango, CO 81301
(970) 247-0111

SW 7 Rainbow Hot Springs
N/A

SW 8 The Spring Inn
P.O. Box 1799
165 Hot Springs Boulevard
Pagosa Springs, CO 81147
(970) 264-4168; or (800) 225-0934;
    FAX: (970) 264-4707
www.pagosasprings.net/springinn

SW 9 The Spa Motel
P.O. Box 37
317 Hot Springs Boulevard
Pagosa Springs, CO 81147
(970) 264-5910; or (800) 832-5523
    (Reservations); FAX: (970) 264-2624

SW 10 Splashland Pool
P.O. Box 972
5895 South Highway 17
Alamosa, CO 81101
(719) 589-6307

SW 11 Colorado Alligator Farm
P.O. Box 1052
Alamosa, CO 81101
(719) 589-3032
gatorfrm@rmi.net
www.rmii.com/~gatorfrm

SW 12 Sand Dune Pool
1991 County Road 63
Hooper, CO 81136
(719) 378-2807

SW 13 Mineral Hot Springs
28640 County Road 58EE
Moffat, CO 81143
(719) 256-4328
www.slv.org/saguache/business/
    mineral.htm

SW 14 Valley View Hot Springs
P.O. Box 65
Saguache County Road GG
Villa Grove, CO 81155-0065
(719) 256-4315; FAX: (719) 256-4317
soak@vvhs.com
www.vvhs.com/soak

SW 15 Salida Hot Springs
410 West Rainbow Boulevard
Salida, CO 81201
(719) 539-6738

SW 16 Waunita Hot Springs Ranch
8007 County Road 887
Gunnison, CO 81230
(970) 641-1266
rpringle@csn.net
www.coloradovacation.com/duderanch/
    waunita/index.html

SW 17 Mount Princeton Hot Springs
15870 County Road 162
Nathrop, CO 81236
(719) 395-2361; or (719) 395-2447

SW 18 Cottonwood Hot Springs
18999 County Road 306
Buena Vista, CO 81211
(719) 395-6434; or (719) 395-2102
hotwater@amigo.net
www.westerntravel.com/hot/

Public Agencies and Resources

Grand Mesa, Uncompahgre, and
  Gunnison National Forests
2250 Highway 50
Delta, CO 81416-8723
(970) 874-7691

Routt National Forest
2468 Jackson Street
Laramie, WY 82070-6535
(307) 745-8971; or (307) 745-2300

Pike and San Isabel National Forests
1920 Valley Drive
Pueblo, CO 81008
(719) 545-8738

Arapaho and Roosevelt National Forests
240 West Prospect
Fort Collins, CO 80526
(970) 498-1100

White River National Forest
900 Grand Avenue
Glenwood Springs, CO 81602
(970) 945-3266

San Juan National Forest
701 Camino del Rio
Durango, CO 81301
(970) 247-4874

Rio Grande National Forest
1803 W U.S. Highway 160
Monte Vista, CO 81144
(719) 852-5941

Visitor Map Sales (National Forest,
  Wilderness, and Grassland Maps)
P.O. Box 25127
Lakewood, CO 80225
(303) 275-5350

Colorado State Parks (Department of
  Natural Resources)
1313 Sherman Street, Room 618
Denver, CO 80203
(303) 866-3437

U.S. Department of the Interior—U.S.
  Geological Survey (Topo Maps)
U.S. Branch of Distribution
Box 25286, Building 810
Denver Federal Center
Denver, CO 80225
(800) USA-MAPS
(303) 844-4169; or (303) 202-4700

U.S. Department of the Interior (BLM
  Maps)
Bureau of Land Management—
  Colorado State Office
2850 Youngfield Street
Lakewood, CO 80215-7093
(303) 239-3600

Colorado Geological Survey
1313 Sherman Street, Room 715
Denver, CO 80203
(303) 866-2611

INTERNET ADDRESSES

The following World Wide Web addresses may be useful in learning more about the hot springs not only in Colorado, but in other areas. It is not a comprehensive list of all websites as much as simply a "starter kit" to help you learn more about what else is out there and how to find some hot links to other sites. There is a growing abundance of good information on the internet. It is an extremely useful resource, if you make use of it.

www.soak.net/nav-hs.htm. This is a list of hot springs by state, and includes latitude and longitude information.

www.oit.osshe.edu/~geoheat/directuse/spa/htm#co. Here is a listing of numerous hot springs in a format of productive use, such as for space heating, domestic hot water, and so on, but also includes some other references.

www.wenet.net/~mead/hungygulch/regguidessht.html. This is a fun listing of bed and breakfast places, but also takes in some hot springs and has some neat back-road archeology and geology information.

www.telosnet.com/ov/ov_hotsprings.html. This is a great source of direct information for a limited set of hot springs and includes hot links to other sites.

REFERENCES AND SUGGESTED READING

Below are some of the reference materials I used to collect information, as well as some interesting reading, if you are curious to find out more about the world of geothermal hot springs, their geology, and related history. Once again, this is not a complete list of credits as much as an abridged bibliography and just-for-fun reading list.

Alt, David and Donald Hyndman. *Roadside Geology of Montana.* Missoula, Montana: Mountain Press Publishing, 1986.

Bauer, Carolyn. *Colorado Ghost Towns.* Frederick, Colorado: Renaissance House Publishers, 1987.

Cappa, James A. and H. Thomas Hemborg. *1992–1993 Low Temperature Geothermal Assessment Program, Colorado.* Colorado Geological Survey, Division of Minerals and Geology, 1995.

Barrett and Pearl. *Hydrogeological Data of Thermal Springs and Wells in Colorado.* Information Series 6, Colorado Geological Survey, 1976.

Frazier, Deborah. *Colorado's Hot Springs.* Boulder, Colorado: Pruett Publishing, 1996.

Bischoff, Matt C. *Touring California and Nevada Hot Springs.* Helena, Montana: Falcon Publishing, 1997.

INDEX

ABOUT THE AUTHOR

A native of Montana, Carl Wambach grew up in Missoula, where the wonders of the outdoor world were close at hand. There are numerous hot springs in the area, and they kindled his early interest in natural hot waters. Family snowmobiling trips to the nearby Montana/Idaho border often included a stop at Lolo Hot Springs on the way home, says Wambach. As an enthusiastic outdoorsmen, Carl's travels within Montana and neighboring states often included hot springs destinations.

Although Carl is a mainframe computer software engineer by profession, the outdoors is both his passion and his history. "If it has to do with the outdoors, I live for it," says Wambach. "I love hunting, horses, flying, fast motorcycles, and seeing new places." He has been in more than thirty foreign countries and all but a small handful of the states and provinces, but he believes the American West is truly the last best place.

This guidebook will take you to some places that are well known, but also to unique locations that you will not find on bus tours. The emphasis is to reveal the best of Colorado's hot springs that are available, safe, and recommended to the public. You will find his enthusiasm for hot springs contagious and his writing sparked by the energy that is the hallmark of his lifestyle. Carl writes from his home in Helena, Montana.